ECONOMICS
MADE EASY
AND STIMULATING
NEW & EXPANDED EDITION

John Maynard Keynes

Alfred Marshall

Karl M

Quick Revision Notes & Articles to Stimulate Economic Reasoning

Bertrand Wong

ECONOMICS MADE EASY AND STIMULATING

QUICK REVISION NOTES & ARTICLES TO STIMULATE ECONOMIC REASONING
NEW & EXPANDED EDITION

PREFACE

Today's students are under pressure more than ever before to master their subjects speedily and efficiently in order to perform well.

This book addresses this problem. It should be able to give students of GCE "A" Level Economics a quick, easy and firm grasp of the subject.

The book covers more than the GCE "A" Level Economics syllabus.

The several specially selected articles in the book, a number of which had been published in professional and learned journals such as those of the Royal Economic Society, the British Society of Commerce and the New Internationalist, should stimulate the reader to think analytically about economics, which has greater ramifications in our life than we may think. Such an analytical mental outlook should enable the reader to do well in his economics exam, and, later , in his business life, should he be in business.

For students under time pressure and constraint, this book should be especially useful for quick revision.

Students of other economics exams, such as the BBA, RSA, LCCI, GCE "O" Level or the GRE exams, etc., should also find the book useful.

General readers, e.g., business practitioners, researchers, and even professional economists, should find something of interest and useful in the book.

Very importantly, the book contains some "creative" economics - there are the author 's well-thought solutions to our often dire and seemingly never ending economic woes, i.e., we seem to be always at the mercy of the economy . Perhaps, the author 's solutions would be the answers to the end of all this.

In the last revised edition, an appendix which comprises of important supplementary notes on inflation and unemployment, with suggested solutions, has been incorporated.

For this new and expanded edition, three stimulating, important articles, The Effect Of Technology On The Economy, The Role Of Greed In The Economy and Why Economics Does Not Solve Economic ProblemsAnd What To Do, are added.

The autho r wishes all readers well and good luck, and, of course, happy reading.

Bertrand Wong, Ph.D.(Bus.), Ph.D.(Engrg.),
Certified Professional Manager, PE,
Vice-Chancellor, Research Professor, Eurotech.

ECONOMICS MADE EASY AND STIMULATING
QUICK REVISION NOTES & ARTICLES TO
STIMULATE ECONOMIC REASONING
NEW & EXPANDED EDITION

CONTENTS

QUICK REVISION NOTES

1.	Introduction To Economics	5
2.	Factors Of Production	5
3.	The Role Of The Entrepreneur	5
4.	Scarcity And Choice	6
5.	What Is Opportunity Cost?	6
6.	"Free" Economies, "Controlled" Economies And "Mixed" Economies	6
7.	Production	7
8.	Types Of Production	8
9.	Demand, Supply And Price	10
10.	Elasticity Of Demand	11
11.	Supply	12
12.	The Law Of Diminishing Returns Affects Land (A Factor Of Production)	13
13.	Reasons For Growth Of Firms	14
14.	Economies Of Scale (Advantages Of Large Scale Production)	14
15.	Diseconomies Of Scale (Disadvantages Of Large Scale Production)	15
16.	Returns To Scale	16
17.	Factors Determining Elasticity Of Supply	16
18.	Factors Affecting Supply	16
19.	Pricing	17
20.	Price Fluctuations	18
21.	Total Revenue And Elasticity Of Demand	19
22.	Profits Maximisation	19
23.	What Are The Conditions/Assumptions For Perfect Competition?	20
24.	What Is A Monopoly?	20
25.	Price Determination Under Monopolistic Competition	22
26.	The Mechanics Of Demand And Supply - A Few Examples	25
27.	Competitive Supply And Choice Of Output	27
28.	The Revealed Preference Theory	27
29.	The Theory Of Choice: Indifference-Curve Analysis	28
30.	Price Controls	33
31.	The Supply Curve Of A Competitive Industry	35
32.	The Supply Curve Under Monopoly Conditions	35
33.	Discriminating Monopoly	36
34.	Consumer Surplus And Price Discrimination	36
35.	What Is A Market?	38
36.	Population	39
37.	Location Of Industries	41
38.	Labour	43

39.	Wages And Unions	46
40.	Entrepreneurship	50
41.	Organisation Of Economic Activities	54
42.	Mergers And Acquisitions	63
43.	Sizes Of Business Units	67
44.	Firms And Their Objectives	72
45.	Stakeholders In The Economy	79
46.	Business Finance	84
47.	Public Finance	90
48.	Economic Development	94
49.	Inflation And Unemployment	97
50.	International Trade	99
51.	Money And Price Level	103
52.	National Income Accounting	105
53.	The Economic Role Of Government	106
54.	The Theory Of National Income Determination	108
55.	Money And Financial Markets	114
56.	Economic Activities In General	118
57.	Economic Activities And The Environment	124
58.	Economic Activities: Marketing And Demography	128
59.	Economic Activities And Market Research	133
60.	Keynesian Economics	142
61.	Financial Institutions (In The Singapore Context)	143
62.	General Use Statistics (In The Singapore Context)	151
63.	The Importance Of Economic Theory In Business	153

ARTICLES TO STIMULATE ECONOMIC REASONING

1.	A New Monetary System For Combating Our Economic Ills	159
	(Written by the author and published in a journal of the Royal Economic Society)	
2.	Neo-Economics: We Should Control The Economy And Not Vice Versa	160
	(Written by the author and published in a journal of the Royal Economic Society)	
3.	Dynamics Of An Economic Downturn	161
	(Written by the author and published in a journal of the British Society of Commerce)	
4.	Solution To The Problem Of World Recession	163
	(Written by the author and published in the New Internationalist)	
5.	Should Job-Hopping Be Regarded As A Bane To The Industries?	163
	(Written by the author and published in a British management journal)	
6.	Financing Needs Of Small Industries: Are They Best Served By A Specialised Institution?	164
7.	The Keynesian Theory	169
8.	Economics Should Change With The Times	170
9.	The Effect Of Technology On The Economy	174
10.	The Role Of Greed In The Economy	177
11.	Why Economics Does Not Solve Economic Problems And What To Do	179

APPENDIX: SUPPLEMENTARY NOTES ON INFLATION AND UNEMPLOYMENT

182

Bibliography	185

QUICK REVISION NOTES

1. INTRODUCTION TO ECONOMICS

Great Victorian economist's definition of Economics: "The study of mankind in the everyday business of life."

Dictionary definition: "Study of economies of nations."

(An economy is a system of interrelationship of moneyindustry and employment in a country.)

Economics involves understanding human "wants".

Wants include: food, water , air, clothes, comfortable homes, entertainment, education, transport, and many, many more.

Utility: Something that has usefulness.

Economics is basically the study of how mankind produces utilities to satisfy wants.

For example, thirst is a "want", and water has "utility" because it satisfies this want.

Production Of Utilities: To Satisfy Wants.

Utilities can take the following forms:

(1)   Goods (Tangible items such as food, clothing, housing, furniture, books, cars and TV sets). Consumer Goods. Producer Goods.

(2)   Services (Intangible utilities such as dental treatment, sur gery, entertainment, etc.). Personal Services. Commercial Services.

Production makes use of producer goods and commercial services to create utilities by providing endless flow of consumer goods and personal services.

2. FACTORS OF PRODUCTION

(1)   Land (Resources provided by bounty of nature, eg., agricultural land, mineral resources of the earth, atmospheric gases, products of fields, forests and oceans, and even resources from outer space.)

(2)   Labour (All the human resources of the earth, the physical and mental abilities of the peoples of the world.)

(3)   Capital (Producer goods.)

3. THE ROLE OF THE ENTREPRENEUR

The Concept Of "Supply-side Economics" (Has been dubbed Reaganomics during U.S. President Reagan's term of office):

It means achieving higher and higher productivity in order to solve the country' economic problems.

The Role Of The Entrepreneur

1. Takes initiative in combining factors of production (land, labour and capital) in best possible way to create utilities which will satisfy man's wants.
2. Plays leadership role.
3. Takes risks.
4. Coerced by the profit motive.

4. SCARCITY AND CHOICE

1. We shall never be able to completely satisfy men' s wants, no matter how much we produce.
2. Men's wants develop and extend with every advance of technology.
3. Utilities that can be created are   limited compared with the   insatiable appetites of men. (Resources of the earth are scarce.)
4. Thus, mankind has to exercise some kind of   choice as to what shall be produced and in what quantities.
5. How we make the choice depends on type of society in which we live. (E.g., in a "free-enterprise" society, choice is exercised freely by a wide range of individuals and groups - market forces play freely , advertising and sales promotional activities take sway , and people could "pick and choose" a great variety of utilities.)

5. WHAT IS OPPORTUNITY COST?

1. Making choices has its opportunity costs.
2. Opportunity Cost: Could be regarded as "Alternative Cost."
   It could be regarded as "the cost of a commodity not in money but in terms of the alternative forgone."
3. For example, the student skips lecture to attend a cinema show. The true cost of the cinema visit is the lecture he has missed (and not the few dollars he has spent for the show).

6. "FREE" ECONOMIES, "CONTROLLED" ECONOMIES AND "MIXED" ECONOMIES

1. Economic activity is carried out in a climate which to some extent reflects the political framework of society.

2.   In every nation there is more or less control by Government over economic activities.

3.   The less the governmental control, the freer the economy is.

4.   Remember:
      a)   Totally free enterprise does lead, regrettably, to some abuses.
      b)   It tends to lead to gross inequalities of incomes, and, to various types of monopoly practices.

5.   Hence, political solutions to these injustices, e.g., communist (controlled) economies like China and (previously) the U.S.S.R..

6.   Military solutions do sometimes occur e.g., Ugandan controlled economy

7.   In many countries, a "mixed" economy has evolved.

8.   In a "mixed" economy, there are certain centrally controlled (government controlled) industries and a rich pattern of other "free enterprise" industries.

9.   Best example of "free" economy: the U.S.A..

10.   "Controlled" economies: communist or socialist countries, eg., China and North Korea.

11.   "Mixed" economies: the U.K. and Singapore.

12.   A "mixed" economy is favoured by many because:
      (a)   It is virtually impossible for government (no matter how authoritarian) to supervise every aspect of production.
      (b)   The monopolistic exploitation of the masses in a truly "free" economy is totally unacceptable in our increasingly egalitarian modern world.

7. PRODUCTION

Production - Creation of utilities (products and services) to satisfy wants.

Mass production - Term used to describe any system which aims at producing, with the fewest workers, the greatest output of goods.

The three Ss: (1) Specialisation (2) Simplication (3) S   tandardisation help to greatly increase volume of production.

(1)   Simplication

       Is the process of making a manufactured article as simple and functional as possible.

(2)   Standardisation

       Is the process of making things in standard parts, which can be used in many similar articles.

(3)   Specialisation

       Is the process of achieving increased output through the division of labour.

*Mechanisation, automation and computerisation are possible when a design has been reduced to its simplest and most standardised form.

Modern technology is so advanced that instead of regional specialisation, national specialisation is now a distinct possibility.

Division of labour has moved through following stages:

(1)   Use of individual skills and talents.

(2)   Development of specialised trades.

(3)   Subdivision of these trades into specialised aspects.

(4)   Further subdivision of these aspects into processes.

(5)   Mechanisation and automation of processes.

(6)   Computerised control of automatic processes.

Result:- Large-scale industries as follows:

(1)   Industries develop from the family to village or tribal unit.

(2)   Industries develop from countryside to medieval borough or town.

(3)   Industries develop from town to geographical region.

(4)   Industries develop from regional to national level, with particular countries supplying a major part of world's requirements.

(Division Of Labour: Specialisation within a single industry)

Limitations To Division Of Labour

(1)   There may be little demand for a product (so mass production may be of no use).

(2)   It may not be possible to subdivide a technique beyond a certain point (technical impossibility).

(3)   Producing much through mass production may become very risky , especially when the country's currency may devaluate.

8.   TYPES OF PRODUCTION

(1)   Production Of Goods

    (a)   Primary Production (Production of goods made available by Nature. Man's inheritance of natural wealth.)

        Examples: Coal miner, farmer, tin miner , fisherman, oil driller , lumberjack, etc.

    (b)   Secondary Production (Production of sophisticated products which are derived from the natural primary products.)

        Examples: Electronic engineer, builder, carpenter, tailor, steel worker, refinery technologist, etc.

(2)   Production Of Services (Tertiary Production)

    (a)   Commercial Services

Examples: Retailer, banker, insurance agent, importer, exporter, transport driver, ship's crew, etc.

(b)   Personal Services

Examples: Dentist, doctor, lecturer, detective, entertainer, editor, writer, psychologist, etc.

What Are The Advantages Of Specialisation?

(1)   People are free to choose the work they like.

(2)   The specialist uses the same set of tools all day. (No waste of time due to change of tools between different activities.)

(3)   Constant use of same tools and materials leads to close study of both, resulting in improved equipment and better work methods.

(4)   Specialised production allows work to be broken down into processes, whereby use of machines becomes possible. Machines, unlike people, do not tire or feel bored and could speed up production considerably.

(5)   Specialisation results in workers becoming accustomed to a piece of work (due to repetition). This results in workers acquiring enormous skill in what they do.

Nature Of Specialisation As Follows:

(1)   Specialisation within the Family or Tribal Group (E.g., best potter makes pots for entire village, etc.)

(2)   Specialisation into Trades (Engineers, lawyers, doctors, butchers, bakers, etc.)

(3)   Specialisation into Sub-trades (Spinning and weaving, dyeing and fabric-printing, etc.)

(4)   Specialisation into Processes (Manufacturing processes broken down into a series of separate activities)

Disadvantages Of Specialisation As Follows:

(1)   Production in anticipation of demand may result in overproduction.

(2)   Highly specialised jobs are monotonous.

(3)   Craftsmanship declines.

(4)   Structural unemployment (caused by changes in world demand for a product) and regional unemployment may result.

(5)   Mechanisation, automation and computerisation may result in workers being displaced or retrained for other jobs. This may result in industrial unrest and social discontent.

9. DEMAND, SUPPLY AND PRICE

1) An understanding of the working of market forces (supply and demand) is basic to any study of economics.

2) Supply and demand have first to be studied in a theoretical, "unreal" situation, and once understood, these principles can be applied to "real world" situations to help understand the theory of price determination.

3) Demand = The quantity of a good or service buyers are prepared to buy at a given price.

4) Demand would depend on the following conditions:

   a) Goods or services must have utility.

   b) Buyer must have the means (money) to meet the price.

   c) Buyer must be prepared to use his means to obtain the good or service.

5) Demand schedule = Table showing how much demand there is for a good or service at different price levels.

6) Demand curve = Graphical representation of a demand schedule where price is plotted on the vertical axis and quantity demanded is plotted on the horizontal axis.

7) All demand schedules and curves have the following assumptions:

   a) Income of potential buyers remains the same.

   b) Prices of other goods, which have some connection with the good concerned, remain the same.

   c) Tastes of buyers and fashionability of the good remain the same.

   d) Size of market, i.e., number of potential buyers, remains the same.

8) In other words, a demand schedule or curve shows how demand would react to a change in price only - all other possible variables affecting the buying situation are assumed to be unchanged.

9) Normal demand - Most goods follow general rule that if price goes up, less will be demanded and if price goes down, more will be demanded. This is known as normal demand. (Demand curve slopes downward from left to right).

10) Exceptional demand - Demand for some commodities decreases when prices fall. These are inferior goods - they are bought only because buyers cannot afford better alternatives, e.g., bus travel. On the other hand, demand may rise when price goes up as buyers expect further price rises, e.g., shares.

11) Extension of demand = Increase in quantity demanded resulting from a change in price.

12) Contraction of demand = Decrease in quantity demanded resulting from a change in price.

13) Shift in demand = Situation where basic assumptions on which demand schedule/curve rests are altered (e.g., income of potential buyers increases), resulting in buyers buying more at all price levels. (A new demand curve is drawn.)

10. ELASTICITY OF DEMAND

1) Elasticity of demand = Measure of extent to which quantity demanded varies when one of the factors affecting demand varies.

2) Price elasticity of demand = Extent to which demand for a commodity varies when price varies =

$$\frac{\% \text{ change in quantity demanded}}{\% \text{ change in price}}$$

3) Income elasticity of demand = Extent to which demand for a commodity varies when income of potential buyers varies =

$$\frac{\% \text{ change in quantity demanded}}{\% \text{ change in income}}$$

4) Cross elasticity of demand = Extent to which demand for one particular commodity varies when price of another commodity varies =

$$\frac{\% \text{ change in quantity demanded for commodity X}}{\% \text{ change in price of commodity Y}}$$

5) All measurement of elasticity gives a figure ranging from 0 to infinity.

6) 0 elasticity = No response in quantity demanded when there is a change in the other variable being measured.

7) Infinite elasticity = Infinitely large change in demand for a commodity when there is the smallest possible change in the other variable being measured.

8) Elasticity of demand < 1 = Inelastic demand

9) Elasticity of demand > 1 = Elastic demand

10) Elasticity of demand = 1 = Unitary elasticity (E.g., 5% change in income of would-be buyers of sweets results in a 5% change in demand for sweets.)

11) Complementary demand = Situation where demand for one commodity affects demand for another commodity , e.g., demand for tennis rackets results in demand for tennis balls (Joint demand.)

12) Competitive demand = The situation where a change in demand for one commodity affects the demand for the other in the opposite way when the 2 commodities are close substitutes (E.g., an increase in demand for 'pop' cassettes results in decrease in demand for 'pop' records.)

13) Derived demand = Situation where demand for a commodity, especially a raw material, depends on the demand for the final product, e.g., bauxite and tin.

14) Composite demand = Situation whereby a commodity has several different uses and therefore there will be several markets making up total demand, e.g., steel.

15) Factors Determining Price Elasticity Of Demand

    a) Proportion of income spent on commodity. (20% increase in price of matches will have less effect on demand than a 20% increase in price of coffee).

    b) Extent to which commodity is regarded as essential. (Necessity?)

    c) Availability of substitutes or acceptable alternatives for commodity.

    d) Durability of commodity . (2nd. hand cars and new clothes versus school textbooks).

    e) Consumer taste. (Religious, social and economic pressures which influence choice, e.g., fashion, effect of advertising, etc.)

    f) Income of consumer. (Who can and who cannot afford luxuries?)

16) Scale of preferences = Levels of satisfaction for commodities.

17) Marginal utility = Satisfaction enjoyed for additional unit of good

11. SUPPLY

1) Supply = Quantity of a good or service which sellers are prepared to sell at a given price.

2) Market supply = Situation whereby supply cannot be increased at all, e.g., apples on a street trader's barrow.

3) Short-term supply = Situation whereby an increase in supply is made possible by drawing on easily available sources, e.g., the street trader buying more apples from a wholesaler or farmer.

4) Long-term supply = Situation whereby increase in supply is made possible by major changes in resources or technology, e.g., planting new orchards.

5) Supply schedule = Table showing how much supply there is of a good or service at different price levels (usually short-term supply).

6) Supply curve = Graphical representation of supply schedule. (Price is plotted on vertical axis. Quantity supplied is plotted on horizontal axis.)

7) All short-term supply schedules and curves assume following:-

    a) Costs of production, including wages, will not vary outside known limits.

    b) Technology remains the same.

    c) Number and capacity of potential supplies remain the same.

    d) Taxes or subsidies relating to the good or service remain the same.

8) Normal supply = Situation whereby if selling price of commodity goes up quantity supplied will increase. (Supply curve slopes upward from left to right.)

9) Extension of supply = Situation whereby there is an increase in quantity supplied due to a change in price.

10) Contraction of supply = Situation whereby there is a decrease in quantity supplied due to a change in price.

11) Shift in supply = Situation whereby if basic assumptions on which the supply schedule/curve rests are altered, then a new curve is drawn. (E.g., if raw material prices increase, producers may of fer less for sale at all price levels.)

12) Price elasticity of supply = Extent to which supply of a commodity varies

when price varies = $\dfrac{\% \text{ change in quantity supplied}}{\% \text{ change in price}}$

13) Practical Uses Of Price Elasticity Of Supply, As Follows:

a) Manufacturers who buy components from several small suppliers will want to estimate how much they need to offer these suppliers if they want to increase production.

b) If the government of fers a subsidy to a company they will want to gauge the company's potential increase in production.

12. THE LAW OF DIMINISHING RETURNS AFFECTS LAND (A FACTOR OF PRODUCTION)

1) The addition of further quantities of labour or capital to Land would sooner or later result in diminishing returns, i.e., less output per unit of labour or capital applied.

2) Look at diagram below:

Area of land (in acres)	Weight of fertilizer used (in cwts.)	Output of potatoes (in tons)	Increase in output over untreated land	Marginal output (i.e., extra output achieved by each cwt. used)
1	-	5	-	-
1	1	6	1	1
1	2	8	3	2
1	3	10.5	5.5	2.5
1	*4	11.5	6.5	1
1	5	9	4	-2.5

*At this point, the fertilizer has become too concentrated. <u>Maximum output</u> is achieved. But marginal output has begun to decline.

13

(i)   Untreated, the land yields 5 tons per acre.

(ii) Output rises when successive increments of fertilizer are added.

(iii) Notice that the 4th. sack of fertiliser only yields a marginal output of 1 ton (maximum output).

13. REASONS FOR GROWTH OF FIRMS

(1) Larger firms tend to be more efficient - economies of large scale production.

(2) Large firms may establish a dominant position (approaching monopoly) in the market.

(3) Firms producing many products and operating in many different markets reduce risk of a fall in demand for one product (don't put all your eggs in one basket).

Firms can grow by:-

(a) Internal expansion to increase production (natural growth).

(b) Merging or taking over through:

    (i)   Vertical Integration -

    One firm combines with another at a different stage of production, e.g., tyre firm buying a rubber plantation (backward integration), car producer setting up dealerships (forward integration).

    (ii) Horizontal Integration -

    One firm combines with another at same stage of production (economies of large scale production or greater market dominance).

    (iii) Lateral Integration -

    Combining of firms which might have common sources of raw materials or market outlets but are not in direct competition, e.g., Schweppes and Cadbury's.

14. ECONOMIES OF SCALE (ADVANTAGES OF LARGE SCALE PRODUCTION)

(A) Technical or physical economies:

    (i)   Output increases, while labour cost per unit decreases.

    (ii) Increase in volume of machinery and equipment requires less than proportional increase in materials, e.g., steel required for a 500 gallon vat and for a 1,000 gallon vat.

    (iii) Using modern efficient machinery may be more worthwhile.

    (iv) Research and development (R&D) activities may be more worthwhile.

    (v)   Where different stages of production have different optimum levels, matching and better utilisation of different equipment are possible.

(B) Marketing economies:

    (i)   Bulk buying often reduces unit cost and sometimes the bulk buyer can dictate standards of quality.

    (ii)   Selling costs, such as advertising and deliveries, have a lower average cost if spread over a large number of units.

    (iii) Expert buyers and salesmen may be employed. (Easier to attract such employees. More worthwhile to employ them - they probably demand relatively high salaries.)

(C) Financial economies:

    (i)   Large firms may often borrow at lower interest rates than small firms.

    (ii)   They have more sources of finances, including the Stock Exchange, available.

(D) Risk-bearing economies:

    (i)   Demand in international or national markets is less likely to fluctuate than in small, local markets.

    (ii)   Large organisations may have the resources to withstand bad times caused by broken contracts, strikes, bad weather, etc..

    (iii) Insurance premiums do not rise in proportion to the sum insured.

(E) Administrative economies:

    (i)   As production increases, management and supervision do not have to increase at the same rate.

    (ii)   Large organisations which have many production plants or selling outlets may have one central administrative unit (head office).

    (iii) Efficient, though expensive systems, e.g., computers, microfilm, electronic data processing, etc., may be used in large firms.

15. DISECONOMIES OF SCALE (DISADVANTAGES OF LARGE SCALE PRODUCTION)

    (i)   Organisational Problems. Too many layers of management may result in 'red-tape', slowing down the decision making process or failing to correct errors quickly.

    (ii)   Production Problems. Expensive machinery may be idle if sales orders do not match capacity.

    (iii) Labour Relations. Industrial unrest, leading to strikes and other action, is more likely to occur in lar ge organisations. (Managers tend to be more impersonal.)

(iv)   Customer Relations. Impersonal attitudes of employees may lose sales.

Costs

(1)   Total Costs = Fixed Costs (E.g., rent, rates, interest on loans, etc.) Variable Costs (E.g., raw materials and labour)

(2)   Average Cost (Unit Cost) = Total Cost ÷ Output

(3)   Point Of Lowest Average Cost = Optimum (Most Efficient) Output Level

(4)   Marginal Cost = Extra Cost Incurred/Saved If Output Is Increased/Decreased By One Unit = Average Cost At The Optimum Output Level

16. RETURNS TO SCALE

Returns to scale = Returns achieved when an existing combination of factors is increased so as to change the scale of the enterprise.

a)   Constant returns to scale =   The situation when output increases in the same proportion as the increase in the scale of production.

b)   Increasing returns to scale =The situation when output increases in greater proportion than the increase in the scale of production.

c)   Decreasing returns to scale =The situation when output increases in lower proportion than the increase in the scale of production.

Producers will need to know the change in supply which will result.

17. FACTORS DETERMINING ELASTICITY OF SUPPLY

(1)   Extent to which capital and other resources are being used. (If there is spare productive capacity output may be easily increased in response to a price increase.)

(2)   Availability of all the resources needed in production of a commodity.

(3)   Type of equipment needed in production. (T wo years to put up a new building. 10 days to switch production from skirts to blouses.)

(4)   When an entrepreneur can divert supplies to market ofering best rewards, as when he produces for several different markets.

(5)   When a supplier can turn production over easily from unprofitable lines to more profitable ones, as when he produces a variety of products.

(6)   When the costs of entering the industry or the losses sufered by leaving it are small (hawker versus manufacturer with specific capital assets).

18. FACTORS AFFECTING SUPPLY

(1)   Price of the commodity.

(2)   Conditions of supply (costs of production, state of technological development, natural influences and abnormal political influences).

(1) Price mechanism decides what goods shall be produced and to whom they shall be supplied.

(2) It is a self-regulating mechanism which sees to it that the market supplies enough to satisfy demand.

(3) It would be ideal if market is perfectly free.

(4) In reality, this is not so - consumers' choice could be influenced by advertising, there could be governmental and legislative influences (taxation, price controls, etc.).

(5) Prices are fixed in market by interaction of the forces of supply and demand.

(6) Market = Place where buyers and sellers come together.

(7) Market demand = The total demand effect of all individual buyers combined together.

(8) Market supply = The total supply ef fect of all individual producers combined together.

(9) It is usually assumed that buyers behave independently of each other and each buyer is unable to affect the determination of market price.

(10) It is normally assumed that suppliers may affect price, e.g., in the case of monopoly.

(11) Equilibrium price = The price in a market where the quantity demanded is equal to the quantity supplied, as shown below:

   (i) At price P consumers demand quantity Q. The industry is prepared to supply same amount.

   (ii) If price > P, there will be excessive supply. Sellers will be left with unsold goods.

   (iii) If price < P, buyers will not get all that they want. There will be insufficient supply.

   (iv) When there is shift in demand or supply, new conditions will be in force. A new equilibrium price will come about.

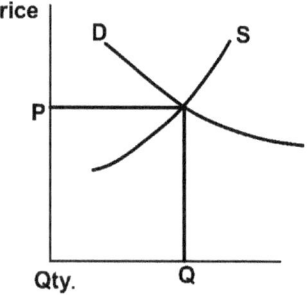

(12) Market price = Short-term equilibrium price decided from day to day in market-place as a result of short-term influences.

(13) Normal price = Long-run equilibrium price.

(14) Entrepreneurs will produce what is necessary to meet demand, if the following conditions exist in market:

(i)   Prices of other goods are not changing particularly.

(ii)   Income of buyers is stable.

(iii) Changes in the number of buyers and their scales of preference are not great.

(15) The following conditions of supply should also exist:

(i)   Prices of raw materials should be stable.

(ii)   Wages and interest rates should be reasonably stable.

20. PRICE FLUCTUATIONS

(1) Price fluctuation - a source of inconvenience to both producers and consumers.

(2) Highly organised markets in market economies (as distinct from planned economies) are developed for the object of smoothing out price fluctuations.

(3) Generally, prices of primary products fluctuate more than prices of secondary products - agricultural products susceptible to interruptions of supply due to bad weather crop diseases, etc. - also tend to be carried long distances to market, so that they are peculiarly susceptible to delays due to strikes, wars, or rumours of wars.

(4) A few examples in price fluctuation as follows:-

(a) (i)   Supply shifts from S1 to S2, caused, e.g., by an increase in wage costs.

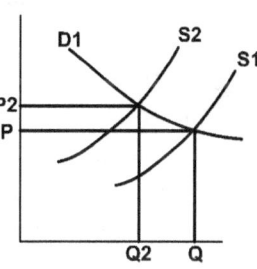

     (ii)   Quantity supplied drops from Q to Q2.

     (iii) Price increases from P to P2.

     (iv) P2 is the <u>new equilibrium price.</u> Q2 is the new equilibrium quantity.

(b) (i)   Demand shifts from D1 to D2, caused, e.g., by an increase in incomes of buyers.

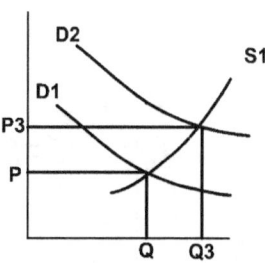

     (ii)   Quantity supplied increases from Q to Q3.

     (iii) Price increases from P to P3.

     (iv) P3 is the <u>new equilibrium price.</u> Q3 is the new equilibrium quantity

21. TOTAL REVENUE AND ELASTICITY OF DEMAND

(1) Total Revenue = Amount spent by consumers on entrepreneur's product = Product unit price x quantity sold.

(2) Changes in price affect total revenue.

(3) If entrepreneur cuts price, will it lower his total revenue?

(4) It depends on the product's elasticity of demand.

(5) If demand is elastic, quantity sold increases more than proportionately and, total revenue will rise.

(6) If demand is inelastic, a price cut will reduce the amount spent by the consumer on his product, and, total revenue will fall (e.g., inferior goods).

Hedging - buying or selling "futures" (ordering or selling in advance), to protect against future increase in price in items purchased or future drop in price of items sold.

(7) Average Revenue = $\dfrac{\text{Total Revenue}}{\text{Quantity Sold}}$ = Price

(8) Marginal Revenue = Revenue received from last unit sold (increment to total revenue).

Note: In perfect competition, the demand curve facing the firm is perfectly elastic, and: Average Revenue = Marginal Revenue = Price (this being basically different from a monopoly situation).

22. PROFITS MAXIMISATION

(1) Every firm is assumed to be trying to maximise profits.

(2) It will increase output up to point at which addition to cost = addition to sales revenue (from the sale of the last good produced).

(3) Normal profit = Profit which keeps number of firms in the industry in equilibrium (when relatively little or no firms enter or leave the industry).

(4) See diagram below:

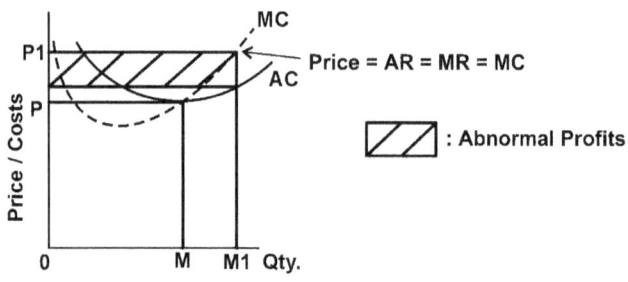

(i)   Optimum output (Output which maximises profit) = Output when: Marginal Cost = Average Cost. (In diagram above, there is no point in producing less than output <u>O M</u> or more).

(ii)   In diagram above, <u>a general increase in demand raises price</u> to P1.

(iii)   Then, each firm will increase output to point at which MC = MR = Price (to O M1).

(iv)   At output O M1, however, Average Revenue = Price, P1, is <u>above</u> Average Cost, and, <u>Abnormal Profits</u> are being earned.

(v)   Other firms will now be encouraged to enter the industry.

(vi)   The increased supply will force down the price to a point where the industry is in equilibrium again (after some firms leave the industry resulting in: Quantity Supplied = Quantity Demanded).

23. WHAT ARE THE CONDITIONS/ASSUMPTIONS FOR PERFECT COMPETITION?

(1)   The firm is small and is one of a large number of other similar companies which make up the total output of an industry, e.g., shoes.

(2)   The firm's products are similar to those produced by all other firms so that consumers have no preference for any particular firm's shoes.

(3)   As the firm is small, it cannot on its own influence total supply of the product, or, the price of the product, by varying its own output. It takes the market price as given.

(4)   As buyers are indifferent as between sellers, in conditions of perfect competition the demand for product of an individual firm is <u>perfectly elastic</u> (horizontal demand curve). The demand curve facing the industry as a whole is <u>normal</u> (sloping down from left to right). (Absence of friction in market.)

(5)   The firm will try to maximise profits. It will try to <u>equate marginal cost with marginal revenue</u>.

(6)   Buyers and sellers have perfect knowledge of the market.

(7)   No buyer or seller receives any preferential treatment.

<u>NOTE</u>: *As a rule some <u>imperfections</u> exist in the market, usually because goods have been "branded" to make them artificially different from similar goods. (This situation is called <u>imperfect competition</u> or <u>monopolistic competition</u>.)*

24. WHAT IS A MONOPOLY?

1)   Monopoly = Situation whereby supply is provided by only one person or firm.

2)   Monopoly can exist only where product being supplied has no close

substitutes and the supplier, for some reason, is able to exclude other firms from producing it.

3) The following conditions may lead to monopolies:

(a) Personal supply by a specialist or talented individual. (E.g., hair stylists and fashion designers.)

(b) Supply under patent right or copyright. (E.g., inventors, authors and composers have legal rights to enjoy fruits of their labours for some period of time, and they are protected from infringement of these rights by others by their patents/copyrights.)

(c) Natural monopolies, e.g., control of natural resources such as coal mines, oil wells or mineral deposits, and, control of expensive capital assets which are socially undesirable to duplicate, e.g., water pipelines and railway lines.

(d) Where large-scale enterprises enjoying economies of scale exist, making it difficult for competitors to enter that industry, for to do so they must be comparable in scale with the efficient firms already established. (Danger of excess capacity in industry/waste of capital. Possibility of cartels.)

(e) Where the product stands out or is well-established, e.g., Kellog's corn flakes and Panadol.

(f) Where the supplier enjoys an excellent reputation and has the good will of customers.

(g) Where it is sanctioned by Acts of Parliament, e.g., nationalisation such as that pertaining to postal services and telecommunications.

(4) Monopolies are not favoured for the following reasons:

(a) They can result in high prices.

(b) Lack of competition often adversely affects quality, service and research and development (R&D).

(5) However, if supervised so as to ensure that the consumer is not exploited, monopolies can enjoy the following economic advantages:

(a) Economies of scale can result.

(b) Wasteful competition is eliminated.

(c) Excess capacity is avoided.

(6) In real life, monopolies are relatively rare, due to following reasons:

(a) There are few suppliers in sole control of raw materials.

(b) Patent rights exist only for limited periods.

(7) Thus, it is difficult for suppliers to keep other suppliers from entering the industry to compete with them.

(8) It is more usual to have "monopolistic competition" (whereby elements of monopoly exist alongside elements of competition).

(9) In monopolistic competition, the industry consists of several firms making almost identical products, each an almost perfect substitute for the other.

(10) Characteristics of monopolistic competition are as follows:

   (a) Product is not homogeneous (differentiated by 'brand names' into a number of different products, each not quite a perfect substitute for the other - producers can char ge different prices and still sell the dearer items).

   (b) There are several suppliers and entry to the industry is still possible. (There can be quite severe competition between products.)

   (c) Heavy expenditure on advertising (informative advertising and persuasive advertising).

(11) Oligopoly = Situation where the product or service is supplied by a small number of firms.

   (a) The activities and policies of each firm are determined by the expected reactions of each to the activities of the others.

   (b) Examples: car manufacturers, oil companies and banks.

   (c) The major problem of the oligopolist is not only profit, but also to maintain his share of the market.

(12) Price System in Free Economy (Capitalist System)

   (i) Price system provides for automatic allocation of economic resources.

   (ii) In practice, because competition is far from perfect, this allocation is not always so automatic or efficient.

(13) Price System in Planned Economy

   (i) Prices are fixed.

   (ii) Demand and supply are not allowed to influence or be influenced by movements in price.

   (iii) Production is strictly controlled.

   (iv) Allocation of all resources is organised centrally.

25. PRICE DETERMINATION UNDER MONOPOLISTIC COMPETTION

1) In perfect competition, the low-cost firm enjoys super-profits in the short run.

2) In the long run new firms entering the industry will lower the price and compete away these super-profits.

3) But, with monopoly conditions, the monopolist is able to maintain his

short-run position into the long term because he can prevent new firms from entering the industry.

4) With monopolistic competition the supplier of branded goods cannot prevent new firms entering the industry, but they <u>cannot enter it and sell his particular brand</u>.

5) See diagram below for price determination under monopolistic competition:

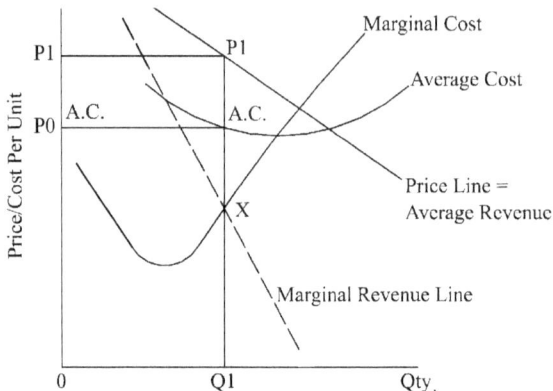

(i) Marginal-cost curve cuts marginal-revenue curve at X, well below the price line.

(ii) Output ceases at this point with an output of O Q1.

(iii) Price is decided by the point where a line from Q1, parallel to the price axis, cuts the price line, at price P1 P1.

(iv) The entrepreneur will earn revenue of O Q1 P1 P1 at a cost (including normal profit) of O Q1 A.C. A.C..

(v) He is therefore earning <u>super-profits</u> of A.C. P1 P1 A.C..

(vi) But, these super-profits will not be competed away (as they would in competitive conditions), because the lucky man is a <u>monopolist</u>.

(vii) The above diagram <u>also</u> represents the <u>short-run position of a firm in monopolistic competition</u>.

(viii) New firms will be attracted into the industry selling the same goods in a differentiated form.

(ix) The new supplier or suppliers will have to be aggressive in advertising and pricing policies in order to compete with the established brand.

(x) To the extent that they are successful there will be a change in the conditions of demand.

(xi) Result of this competition: The demand curve for the supplier of the established brand will <u>shift to the left</u>, i.e., there will be a decrease in demand.

(xii) The marginal-revenue line will also move to the left, and, some of the entrepreneur's super-profits will be competed away.

6) Increasingly monopolistic competition is becoming the characteristic feature of free-enterprise market economies, as far as the consumer is concerned.

7) Perfectly competitive markets may persist to facilitate the bulk handling of primary commodities, but fewer and fewer of such primary products reach the ultimate consumer.

8) The preparation of foods in hygienic pre-packed branded forms, the elimination of personal service in retail trade, the increased standardisation of products, and, the indif ference of af fluent people to minor price differences, all give monopolistic competition great advantages as a method of production.

9) Note following points about monopolistic competition:-

   (i) The competitive monopolist would always aim to preserve his monopoly position. (By attempting to find endless succession of real, or imaginary, improvements in his product, e.g., addition of unnecessary foam to household cleaners, changing the length of cigarettes and cigars, and, endless redesigning of external trimmings on motor vehicles to make them 'new'models. Or, by adding genuine improvements which are beneficial to the consumer, e.g., new types of tyres, braking systems better lighting and design features which improve safety, efficiency of operation, comfort, and convenience have been introduced by motorcar manufacturers as part of the process of presenting an old vehicle in a new form).

   (ii) The industry will usually be operating at less than the optimum. (I.e., there will always be excess capacity in the industry. Active product differention will enable the entrepreneur to operate nearer the optimum while still enjoying super-profits.)

   (iii) Non-price competition is characteristic of monopolistic competition. (Cost of laying down production lines is great. Role of advertising - informative and persuasive.)

10) See diagram below for the long-run position of a supplier under monopolistic competition:

   (i) Owing to changed conditions of demand, the demand curve has moved so far to the left that it has become tangential to (only just touching) the Average Cost cur-ve.

   (ii) At this point, all super-profits are competed away The firm is making normal profits only.

   (iii) There is now excess capacity in the industry.

   (iv) The supplier could increase output to optimum level of minimum average cost at O Q2, and, decrease unit costs by doing so.

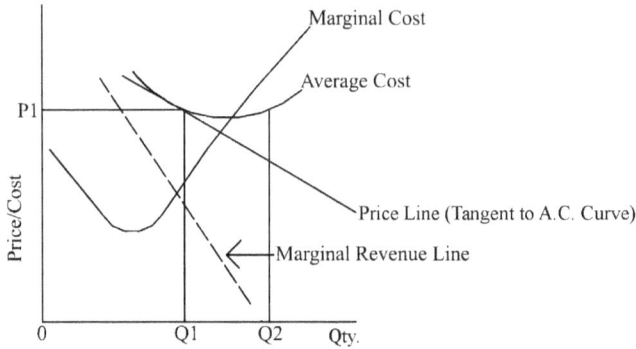

(v) But, the marginal revenue would decrease even more, leaving him worse off.

(vi) It is therefore a feature of monopolistic competition that excess capacity exists in the industry in the long run (i.e., the competitive monopolist will not produce at the optimum level, as it is not to his advantage to do so).

26. THE MECHANICS OF DEMAND AND SUPPLY - A FEW EXAMPLES

1) Joint Demand - Motor Cars And Petrol:

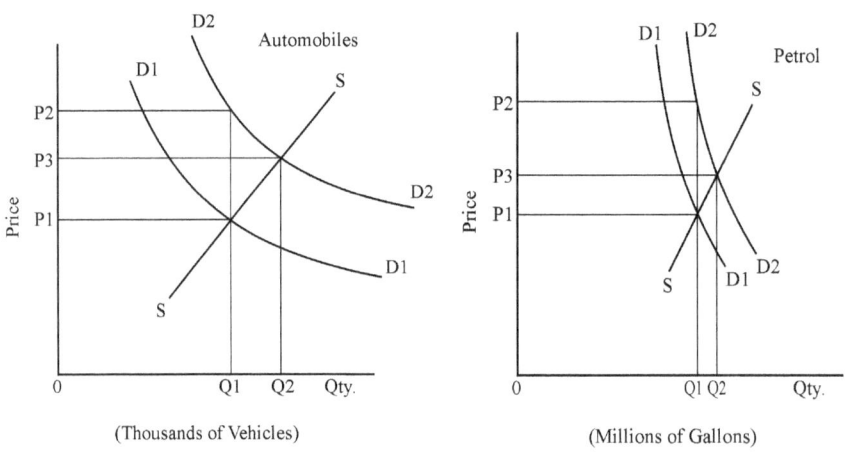

(Thousands of Vehicles)   (Millions of Gallons)

(a) The change from D1 to D2 represents a similar proportional increase over D1, in each case.

(b) It is assumed that the supply of automobiles tends to be elastic and that the supply of petrol tends to be inelastic. Therefore, the change in demand affects the price of the two goods differently.

(c) Both products eventually settle at price, P3, and, quantity, Q2.

(d) Because of the dif ferent elasticities of supply of automobiles and petrol, the price of automobiles rises by a <u>lower percentage</u> than the price of petrol.

2) <u>Competitive Demand Of Butter And Margarine:</u>

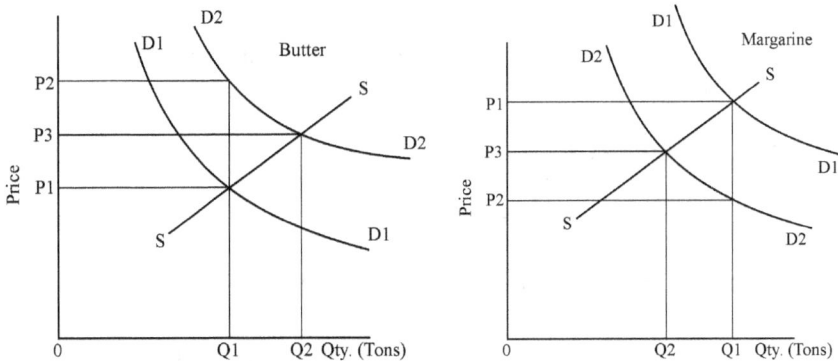

(a) Because of some change in the conditions of demand, butter is more strongly demanded.

(b) The price of butter rises from P1 to P2, settling at P3 as the quantity supplied extends from Q1 to Q2.

(c) Margarine is presently not demanded strongly , as butter has substituted it.

(d) The price of mar garine falls from P1 to P2, but recovers to P3 as supply contracts from Q1 to Q2.

3) <u>Joint Supply - Hides And Beef:</u>

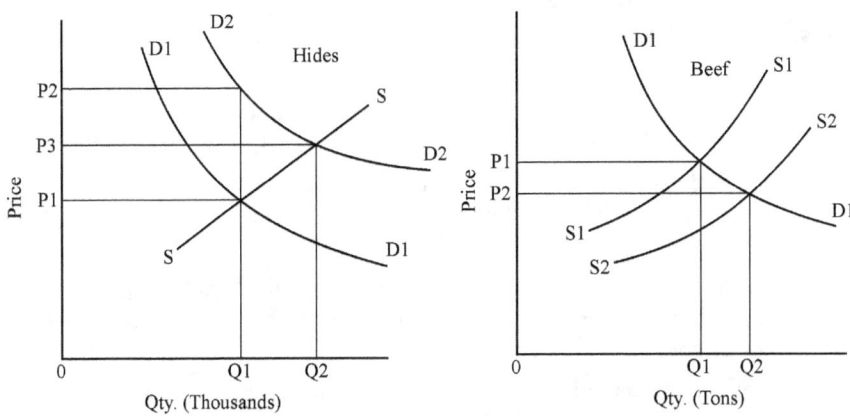

(a) A change in demand for leather goods increases the demand for hides.

(b) Demand for hides now moves from D1 D1 to D2 D2 (shift in demand). Supply extends to Q2. Price settles at P3.

(c)   The increased output of hides throws more beef into the market.

(d)   The supply of beef now shifts from S1 S1 to S2 S2. But, there is no increase in the demand for beef.

(e)   The oversupply of beef now pushes the price of beef down to P2 (from P1).

(f)   As the price of beef falls to P2, the demand for beef extends (increases) to absorb the extra output.

27. COMPETITIVE SUPPLY AND CHOICE OF OUTPUT

1)   The supply of certain goods follows naturally from circumstances beyond man's control.

2)   A rice-grower, e.g., cannot suddenly switch to growing bananas or coffee beans.

3)   E.g., when a farmer grows wheat on a piece of land, he foregoes the opportunity of rearing cattle (for milk and beef) on the same piece of land.

4)   Entrepreneurs choose between different products to produce.

5)   On a broader view, the competition between entrepreneurs for factors of production (land, labour and capital) makes choice essential.

6)   We have to choose not only between individual products but also between broad alternative policies. (Shall we have more material goods or more leisure, more education or more food, more travel or more stylish clothes?)

7)   The factors of production we have are limited.We cannot have everything. We have to choose.

28. THE REVEALED PREFERENCE THEORY

1)   The theory holds that the preferences which a household has already revealed will give a clue to its behaviour when prices change, and explain what quantity or range of quantities it will demand in the new situation.

2)   This readjustment to a new basket of goods can be explained by dividing the price change into two different parts: (a) the substitution effect (b) the income effect.

3)   Substitution effect as follows - substituting a good which has fall in price for another good, or , substituting a good which has a   rise in price with another good.

4)   Income effect as follows - a change in the price of goods always af fects the real incomes of households, i.e., their income in terms of what can be bought with their money. (A fall in prices increases real incomes.A rise in prices reduces real incomes).

5) The substitution effect is always "non-negative", i.e., it always does what is expected. (It leads a household to buy more of a cheaper product, and can never lead it to buy less. It leads a household to buy less of a dearer product, and can never lead it to buy more.)

6) On the other hand, the income effect may be positive or negative. (When real incomes rise people tend to buy more of most commodities, but with some commodities increased income will enable us to change our way of life, alter our diet, etc., so that less of some goods (the so-called 'inferior goods') are now demanded.)

29. THE THEORY OF CHOICE: INDIFFERENCE-CURVE ANALYSIS

1) Indifference-curve analysis: A useful technique for considering how consumers choose between alternative satisfactions.

2) In indifference-curve analysis, we build up a pattern of indifference curves, each recording a chain of choices between alternatives which yield equal satisfaction.

3) See table below for indifference choices:

	← Other Acceptable Choices →				First Choice	← Other Acceptable Choices →		
Units Of Commodity M	16	12	9	7	5	4	3	2	1
Units Of Commodity N	1	2	3	4	5	7	9	12	16

(N.B.: It is assumed that the combinations of M and N shown yield the consumer equal satisfaction)

4) Note that the consumer would demand greater quantities of N for each succee-ding unit of M surrendered. The above table can be graphically represented as below:

Note: The consumer will be equally satisfied at any point along this curve. At Q1 he purchases 5 units of M and 5 units of N. At Q2 he purchases 7 units of M and 4 units of N. He is indifferent to which he has, as his satisfaction is the same in either case.

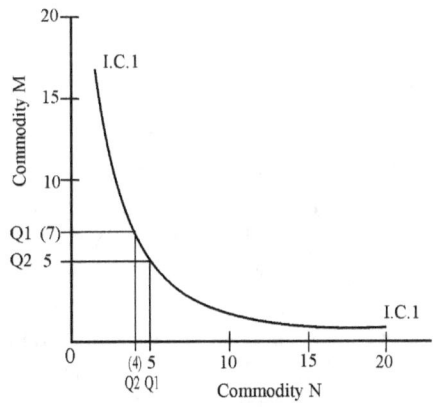

Indifference Curve

5) Further groups of choices at higher levels of satisfaction could be drawn up to give a pattern of indifference curves, as shown below:

Pattern Of Indifference Curves

a) Which of these possible choices will our consumer actually pick?

b) He would naturally like to select a choice on one of the indifference curves a long way away from the original O (since the farther he is from O, the greater the quantities of both pro-ducts he will be able to enjoy, and the greater the satisfaction to be achieved).

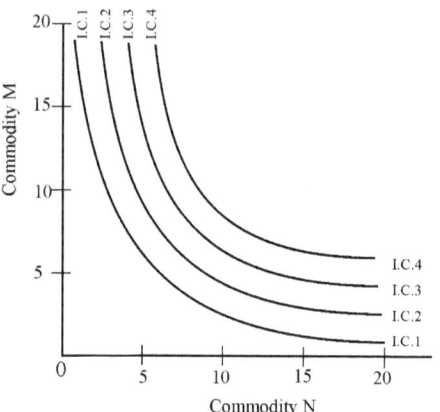

Pattern of Indifference Curves

c) But, his income is limited. The portion of his income to be spent on these two commodities is even more limited.

d) Suppose this portion of his income could buy just 20 units of commo-dity M, or, alternatively, just 14 units of commodity N.

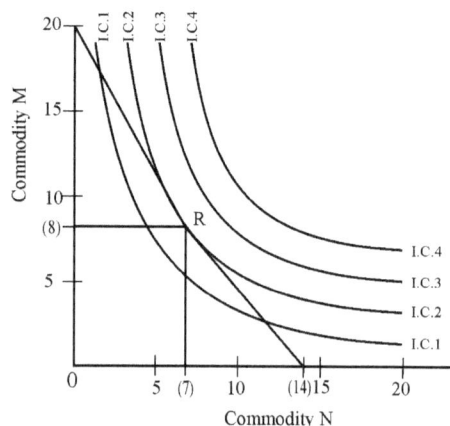

Buying to Achieve Maximum Satisfaction

e) A line joining 20M to 14N, the budget line of the consumer , is shown in diagram below , and indicates the possible combinations of M and N that can be afforded.

f) He can spend this portion of his income in any way he likes. But the choice that is going to yield him the greatest satisfaction is the point on the line PQ which touches the indifference curve farthest from O - this is the point R on I.C.2.

g) His actual choice, i.e., the choice which gives him the greatest satisfaction, will be 8 units of M and 7 units of N.

6) Indifference curves enable us to explain the behaviour of an individual, balancing two commodities one against the other.

7) It is much more sensible to imagine individuals weighing up the satisfaction to be obtained from different combinations of two commodities (as is in the case of "indif ference" analysis, as against measuring the mar ginal utilities of the two commodities).

8) If we wish to imagine the consumer weighing up the satisfaction to be derived from different combinations of many commodities we can make one of the axes in the diagram represent money.i.e., all other commodities.

9) See diagram below for effect of a fall in price (change in the price) of a commodity:

(a) The total money available to consumer is M.

(b) If all this money is spent on the commodity at the starting price, it will buy OC quantity of the commodity.

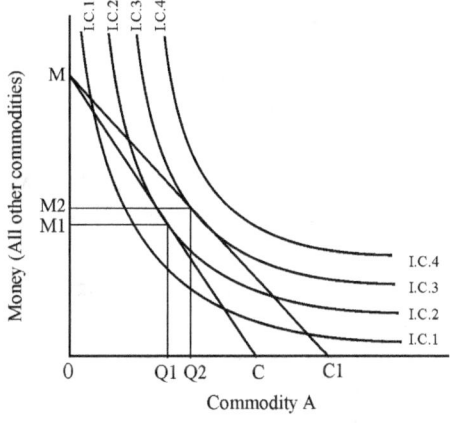

(c) Indifference curve I.C.2 indicates that consumer would like to have any combination of money and goods on that curve.

(d) But, as can be seen, his budget line indicates only one possible choice - he can have O Q1 quantity of the commodity and O M1 amount of money (the rest of the money M1 M being spent to buy the commodity).

(e) When the price of the commodity falls, the money is now enough to buy quantity O C1 of it.

(f) The line M C1 touches the third indifference curve I.C.3.

(g) The consumer will buy more (O Q2 quantity) of the new cheaper commodity, and keep O M2 of the money.

(h) As the indifference curve I.C.3 is farther from O, it is obvious that the consumer now has increased satisfaction from both his purchases (O Q2) and the extra money (O M2) left.

10) See diagram below for the efect of inflation (a fall in the value of money):

(a) In inflation, the income earned rises as fast as, or even faster than, the price of goods.

(b) In this example, let us assume that though higher incomes are being received, the prices of goods are rising proportionately (so that only the same quantity of goods and services can be purchased if total income is spent).

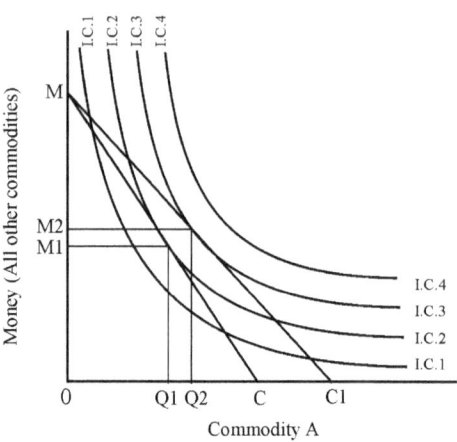

(c) Money incomes have risen from M1 to M2. But, outputs of goods and services have not risen. (This causes prices of goods and services to rise).

(d) The higher income line is tangent to indifference curve I.C.3.

(e) Although real incomes are not higher because the money incomes will buy only the same quantity of real goods, the consumer is deluded into:

(i) buying more of Commodity A (because the extra money in his pocket has less utility than before),

(ii) thinking that the lar ger residue of money (money not spent, i.e., O E2, as against O E1) is "more" in real terms.

(f) The consumer therefore experiences more satisfaction in both real and psychological terms.

11) Diagram below demonstrates the effect of a rise in income:

(a) With income O M1 the consumer can buy O Q1 of commodity A.

(b) With income O M1 he will buy O X1 of commodity A, with a total expenditure of E1 M1, retaining the balance O E1 of his income.This presents him the maximum satisfaction.

(c) When he gets a real increase in income to O M2, he can now buy O Q2 of commodity A.

(d) However, he will again purchase that quantity which maximises his satisfaction. (This point is to be found on indifference curve I.C.4.)

He will purchase O X2 of commodity A for total expenditure of E2 M2, retaining the balance O E2 of his income.

(e) It is obvious that the satisfaction achieved has been increased, which is to be expected when incomes rise.

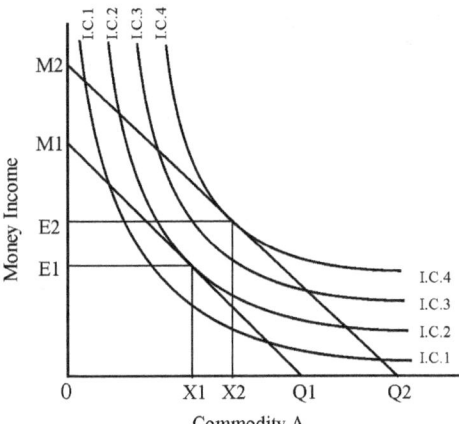

12) The diagram below shows the income and substitution effects on the change in price of a commodity:

(a) In this example, price of commodity A has changed so that more of it can now be bought with the same income.

(b) Instead of purchasing O Q1 of the commodity and keeping O M1 of his income, the consumer now buys O Q3 of the commodity and saves O M3 of his income.

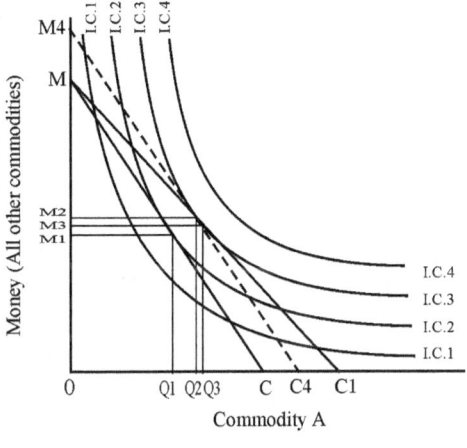

(c) Let us assume that his income has changed enough to buy him the same satisfaction (indifference curve I.C.3) as he is now able to enjoy

(d) There is now a sliding out from the budget line MC a new budget line, M4 C4, parallel to M C.

(e) This new budget line is tangential to the indif ference curve I.C.3, whereby O Q2 of commodityA will be purchased, giving an income saving of O M2.

(f) Thus, the income effect is a change from Q1 to Q2 and from M1 to M2.

(g) The substituition effect is a change from Q2 to Q3 and from M2 to M3.

30. PRICE CONTROLS

1) The price mechanism determines what goods shall be produced and to whom they shall be supplied.

2) It is a self-regulating mechanism which calls on to the market supplies of goods large enough to satisfy the demand.

3) The price mechanism would be a very satisfactory system for distributing "scarce" supplies among customers, if all markets were perfectly free (though, in fact, not all markets are perfectly free).

4) Many goods put on the market would not be demanded at all if people were left alone.

5) It is persuasive advertising that creates demands for such goods (though critics may hold that the creation of artificial "wants" in this way is undesirable as it diverts scarce resources, which could be more usefully employed in other ways, into the production of unnecessary goods).

6) A complaint against the price mechanism are the anti-social overtones inherent in the system which is incapable of responding to anything but demand and supply. (E.g., if addicts demand heroin the market will supply it, and society ought to have a say in such matters.)

7) In real life, however, governments and legislative bodies interfere a good deal in the free play of the price mechanism and manipulate the market to achieve desirable social ends. (E.g., imposing higher taxation which raises effective prices, giving out subsidies which lower ef fective prices, and price controls (physical controls), which dictate maximum and minimum prices.)

8) See diagram below for maximum price controlled: rationing -

   a) When market price is P1, the quantity supplied is Q1.

   b) In this example, the commodity is a basic food in wartime and the market mechanism is enabling the rich to have food while the poor starve.

   c) The government then steps in and sets a maximum limit for the price at P2.

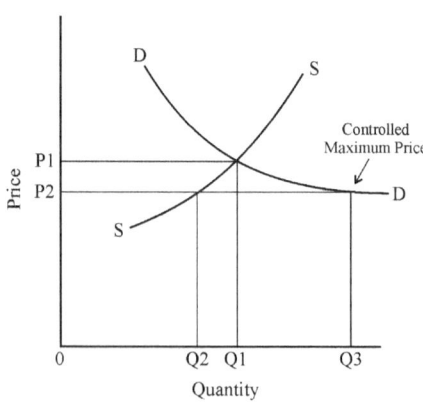

d) At price P2 quantity Q2 is distributed by the suppliers.

e) But the people would like to purchase quantity Q3. (There is a serious shortage in supply. Unscrupulous shopkeepers would keep supplies under the counter for favoured customers - this is unfair).

(f) To ensure everyone gets some of the food supplied, the government then introduces a food rationing system.

9) See diagram below for minimum price controlled: state stockpiling -

(a) When market price is P1 the quantity supplied is Q1.

(b) The government then decrees that prices cannot fall below P2, e.g., to guarantee farm incomes.

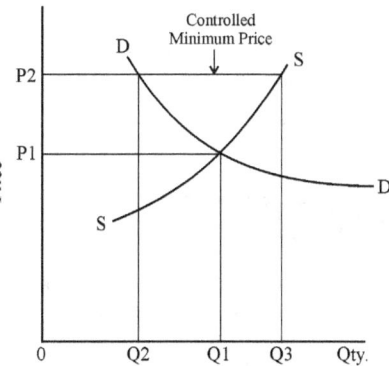

(c) At price P2 the people wish to buy quantity Q2 of the commodity.

(d) But suppliers want to supply quantity Q3.

(e) As the public does not buy the excess quantity, the government has to do so.

(f) The result: Vast stockpiles of food and raw materials are built up which have been purchased with taxpayers' money (by the government).

(g) Sometimes quite ridiculous situations develop, e.g., hungry people may go unfed while granaries are bursting.

(h) Examples:

(i) The U.S. has at times encountered great dificulties because of such stocks and has had to adopt the "soil bank" scheme - this pays farmers when they do not produce, leaving the ground to gain in fertility by lying fallow.

(ii) The Common Market countries also have, from time to time, huge reserves of farm products, e.g., butter and wine.

(i) It pays a firm to produce that output where mar ginal cost rises to equal marginal revenue. (At any point before this the marginal unit will cost less than its sales price, i.e., it will make a profit.)

31. THE SUPPLY CURVE OF A COMPETITIVE INDUSTRY

1) An industry comprises low-cost firms, medium-cost firms and high-cost firms.

2) At low prices only low-cost firms will supply.

3) As prices increase, medium-cost firms will find it possible to produce at a profit and will start up.

4) At very high prices even the high-cost firms enter the industry with some supplies to the market.

5) The supply for a competitive industry is the sum of the quantities supplied by the individual firms.

32. THE SUPPLY CURVE UNDER MONOPOLY CONDITIONS

(1) A supply curve is basically a pictorial representation of the quantities of goods supplied by the industry at certain prices.

(2) In monopoly conditions the sole supplier is not bound by any automatic relationship between supply and price.

(3) The monopolist can manipulate the price by varying the supply if the goods he produces are in inelastic demand, subject to the whim of the monopolist.

(4) The monopolist will still equate marginal cost with marginal revenue, but will never produce a unit if it means a decline in total profit.

(5) He will usually choose to maximise profits (and will produce that output which equates marginal cost with marginal revenue, but may settle for less than maximum profits if he wishes.)

(6) Under monopoly conditions, there is no unique relationship between price and supply. (There is no relationship which follows automatically from a change in demand.)

(7) See diagrams below:

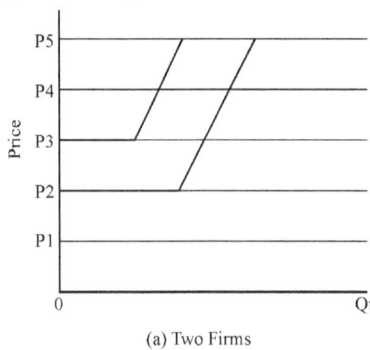

(a) Two Firms

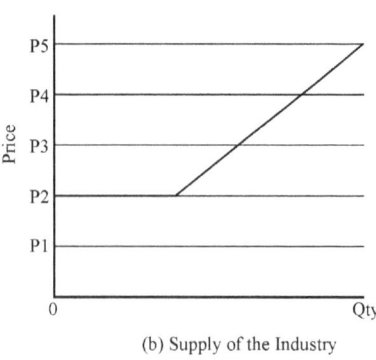

(b) Supply of the Industry

35

(i) The individual supply curves of two firms are shown in (a) above. (In real life, there would be many such firms.)

(ii) The supply curve of the industry is the horizontal addition of the outputs of all the firms in the industry.

(iii) The two firms' outputs (as shown in (a)) have been added in (b) above. (In practice, there would be many such firms, whose outputs are decided by the shape of their marginal-cost curves above minimum average variable cost.)

33. DISCRIMINATING MONOPOLY

(1) A monopolist can sometimes sell the product at different prices to different customers. (E.g., a suit sold in an af fluent area may fetch a better price than a similar suit sold in a less affluent area, cement producers often sell bulk cement at a very much lower price than they sell to retail customers for the same product, railways often char ge special rates to certain customers, etc..)

(2) Price discrimination cannot take place under perfect market conditions.

(3) If price discrimination is to succeed some element of monopoly must exist.

34. CONSUMER SURPLUS AND PRICE DISCRIMINATION

(1) In perfect competition there is only one market and only one market price for each product.

(2) In monopoly or monopolistic competition there are a whole series of prices.

(3) If goods are sold at a price of $1.00, because that price is the only price at which the monopolist's output can be sold, it does not change the fact that some people buying the goods at that price would have been prepared to pay $1.10 or $1.20 or even $2.00.

(4) These people are enjoying a consumer's surplus, i.e., a bonus of satisfaction which results from the monopolist's decision to lower his price and sell a bigger output.

(5) A consumer's surplus represents a loss to the monopolist.

(6) If the monopolist could strike a bar gain with every customer and get that customer to pay what the commodity is worth to him instead of the market price, he would improve his profits. (The monopolist can do this when he sells to different customers at different prices.)

(7) In order to sell to dif ferent customers at dif ferent prices, the following conditions should exist:

(a) It should be possible to keep the "markets" apart. (Physical barriers such as frontiers, the market being too far away from the customer, restrictive trade practices such as contractual fixing of prices, etc..)

(b) The elasticity of demand in the two markets should be different. (No point in offering two different prices if the elasticity of demand of the two groups of customer is the same. It is the refusal of the favoured customer to buy unless the terms are made favourable to him that makes the monopolist offer a cheaper rate, i.e., the favoured customer has a more elastic demand than the unfavoured customer . E.g., a large industrial user of gas might make special arrangements for a preferential rate in return for using this fuel rather than oil or coal, and, cheap-rate electricity at of f-peak hours for domestic heating coerces householders into installing electrical storage heaters rather than other heaters using alternative fuels.)

(8) Result of these discriminating policies:-

(i) A larger volume of output.

(ii) The excess capacity in the monopolist's undertaking is reduced. (He is nearer to the optimum position at which a competitive industry works.)

(iii) Discriminating monopolist now has problem of equating the marginal cost of his entire output with a marginal revenue made up of:

*(a) the marginal revenue to be earned from the consumers in the normal market, and

*(b) the marginal revenue to be earned from the privileged customers.

Note:(a) and (b) are shown in following diagrams as Market I and Market II respectively.

(9) See diagrams below for output of a monopolist when discrimination is possible:-

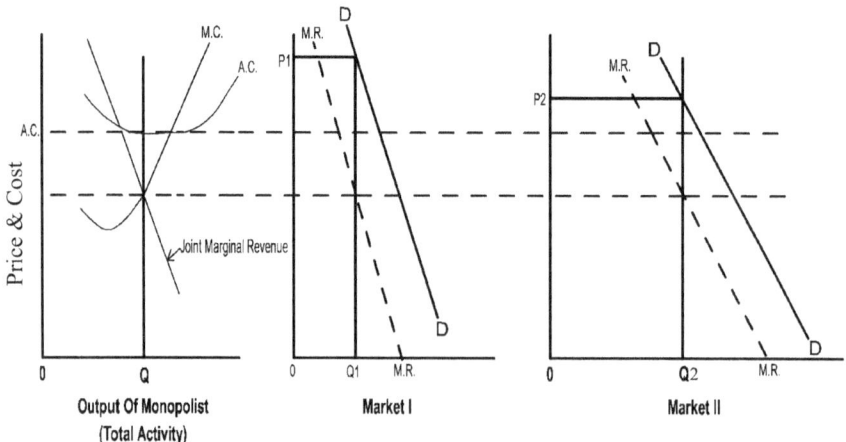

37

(i) The entrepreneur increases output until maginal cost equals marginal revenue.

(ii) That level of cost is carried over into Markets I and II (and in each case cuts the marginal revenue lines 1 and 2 at points which indicate outputs O Q1 and O Q2).

(iii) As shown above, output O Q1 in Market I will be sold at price P1, and, output O Q2 in Market II will be sold at price P2.

(iv) The monopolist is making super-profits in each case, but more so in Market I than Market II. (His discrimination in favour of the market where demand is more elastic depends on his ability to keep the two markets separate.)

35. WHAT IS A MARKET?

(1) It is the place where buyers and sellers come together.

(2) Market demand =The total demand effect of all individual buyers combined together.

(3) It is usually assumed that buyers behave independently of each other and each buyer is unable to affect the determination of market price.

(4) Market supply = The total supply ef fect of all individual producers combined together. It can be assumed that suppliers may afect price, e.g., in the case of monopoly.

(5) What is equilibrium price?

It is the price in a market where the quantity demanded is equal to the quantity supplied.

(6) This is represented below:

(i) At price P consumers demand quantity Q. The industry is prepared to supply same amount.

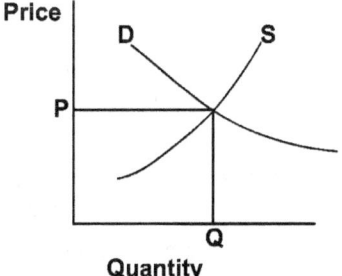

(ii) If price > P, there will be excess supply. Sellers will be left with unsold goods.

(iii) If price < P, buyers will not get all that they want. There will be insufficient supply.

(iv) When there is shift in demand or supply, prices will change accordingly.

36. POPULATION

Population is an important aspect of economics as people are both producers and consumers.

Optimum Population

1) A country with the ideal population size, i.e., optimum population, would experience a fall in its standard of living if the population increases (resulting in over-population) or decreases (resulting in underpopulation).

2) In practice, it is impossible to measure precisely the optimum population of any country, for even if accurate data available, circumstances such as the level of technology and the availability of resources are always changing, thus altering the optimum figure.

3) Therefore, the "optimum population" could only be considered in the most general sense.

Changes In Population

1) Changes in population are affected by the following:-

   i) Increase or decrease in the birth-rate.

   ii) Increase or decrease in the death-rate.

   iii) Changes in the immigration and emigration rates.

Population Measurement

1) The following are the most important measures of population:-

   i) Birth-rate (number of live births per thousand of the population per year).

   ii) Death-rate (number of deaths per thousand of the population per year).

   iii) Net migration (difference between the totals of immigrants and emigrants, with "+" denoting a net increase in the population and "-" denoting a net decrease.

   iv) Age distribution of the population (highlights the changing proportions of young and old people).

Population Problems

1) Aging population (caused by a decrease in the birth-rate, or a decrease in the death-rate, or a combination of both, or a migration of young people).

2) Declining population (caused by the death-rate exceeding the birth-rate, or, emigration being greater than immigration).

3) Increasing population (caused by an increase in the birth-rate, or a decrease in the death-rate, or a combination of both, or an increase in immigration; in modern times, usually associated with an aging population).

Effects Of An Aging Population

1) The proportion of old people increases with the increase in the population

2) The population would become less mobile geographically (older people are less likely to be willing to move around the country) and occupationally (older people are both less willing and less able to adopt new skills and trades).

3) There would be a shift in consumption patterns; goods and services for young people, e.g., adventure holidays and walkmans, would be in less demand, while goods and services for old people, e.g., medical products and chiropody, would be in greater demand; thus, some industries would contract while others expand.

4) Labour would be in short supply; there might be an increase in automation and mechanisation, an increase in real wages and an increase in the retirement age.

5) Attitudes of businessmen and workers might be affected; as older people are generally more conservative, there would be less risk-taking and new investments; there would be less innovation and fewer new products; all this could be the result of either a market with an increasing proportion of old people or a smaller market.

Effects Of An Increasing Population

1) An increased population might lead to an increase in the size of the labour force; if the labour force becomes a higher percentage of the population, this might result in an increase in national output and reduced tax levels, since a smaller dependent population needs less expenditure per tax-payer on pensions and other services.

2) A reduction in the average age of the population would result in an increase in labour mobility geographically and occupationally , less demands for some of the services of the welfare state, e.g., medical benefits and pensions, greater demands for some of the services of the welfare state, e.g., maternal benefits and education, and greater innovation and enterprise (on account of youthful ambition).

3) If the increase in population is due to an increase in the birth-rate, there would be a shift in consumption patterns; markets would be dominated by the needs and wants of young people, and industries would hence be affected.

4) An increased population implies an increased market, which might encourage greater investment in the expectation of greater sales; if firms do not produce enough for the growing market, inflation might occur as excess demand pushes up the prices.

5) If the increase in population happens when the country' s resources are

not fully exploited (under -population), a rise in the standard of living might result.

6) If the rise in population takes place when the country's resources are being fully utilised (optimum population), production patterns would have to change to provide suficient essential goods and services, and, shortages in less essential things would result.

7) The effects of a population increase are unlikely to be the same throughout the whole country - housing problems, traffic congestion and pollution, etc., would vary.

8) An increased population would not automatically lead to an increase in output; if the national output does not increase in the same proportion as the population increase, a fall in the standard of living would result as more people would be sharing the national income cake; this might happen for some time if the increase in population is due to an increase in the birth-rate.

37. LOCATION OF INDUSTRIES

Factors Influencing The Location Of Industries

1) There are various reasons for the location of industries, e.g., the owner establishing a factory in the area where he lives (a non-economic reason).

2) By setting up a business in a particular area, a firm could reduce its production costs (independent of the firms efficiency) simply because of its location in that particular area.

3) There are external economies (advantages) for locating in that particular area.

4) These external economies might take the following forms:-

i) Existence of a skilled, trained labour force in the area.

ii) Existence of a range of subsidiary industries in the area, e.g., firms in the area supporting the companies which have established themselves there and technical colleges and universities in the area running relevant courses and undertaking relevant research in support of the companies or industries established in the area.

iii) Existence of specialist services serving an industry e.g., accounting, warehousing, transporting, banking, legal, advertising and marketing services.

iv) Availability of an efficient transport system in the area, e.g., good roads, railways, airports and seaports.

v) Existence of a large market in the area.

vi) Prestige of the area, which helps in the marketing effort.

vii) Availability of cheap land (which is needed by some industries in large amounts).

Regional Problems (Regional Imbalance)

1) The above factors inter-relate and have a snowball effect - the more the industry concentrates in an area, the more subsidiary firms, specialist services, etc., develop in the area, which would in turn attract more firms in the industry to the area.

2) There could be an uneven pattern of economic growth in different parts of the country, resulting in the following problems:-

   i) High levels of unemployment in a number of regions, with the associated social problems such as poor housing conditions, lack of local amenities and a high crime rate.

   ii) A shift of population to areas of high employment, resulting in social problems such as shortage of housing, schools and health facilities.

   iii) An industry could develop in a particular area where labour is in short supply, resulting in high minimum wages to attract the necessary labour thus increasing production costs, and, wage drift where the actual earnings greatly exceed minimum wage levels through bonus schemes, non-monetary benefits, etc., which also increases production costs.

   iv) An industry concentrating in a particular area could experience external diseconomies (disadvantages), i.e., production costs increase totally independent of the firm' s efficiency - land prices increase and rates increase when land is in short supply , transport costs increase because of trafic congestion and labour costs increase due to the short supply of labour.

Government Policy On The Location Of Industries

1) Though governments realise that firms usually favour locations where production costs are at the lowest levels, they have to consider the economy as a whole and attempt to avoid the problems of imbalance stated above.

2) Governments could adopt compulsion or push measures, e.g., requiring all firms wishing to expand to obtain an Industrial Development Certificate (IDC), the withholding of which by the government means that they not allowed to expand.

3) They could also adopt persuasion or pull measures, i.e., create "artificial" external economies in the form of inducements which would allow a firm to reduce its production costs by locating in a particular area, e.g., the following inducements (direct and indirect):-

   i) Regional employment premiums - a part of the workers' wages is paid by the government.

ii) Training schemes whereby workers are trained at the government's expense.

iii) Availability of factories, purchased or leased, at the most economical rates

iv) Generous grants and tax allowances made available to firms in certain areas when they expand or purchase new equipment.

v) Developing an infrastructure, e.g., an efficient transport system, in certain areas, to encourage firms to locate there.

vi) Grants to local authorities to enable them to attract firms by , e.g., developing town centres, building industrial estates and implementing a housing program.

vii) Carrying out publicity campaigns to get the industries' attention and interest regarding the various attractions and economic advantages of the various regions.

Implications Of Government Intervention

1) Firms which are persuaded to locate in areas where costs are at a minimum enjoy reduced production costs, which could result in exports that are more competitive.

2) The social costs of industries might be reduced because there are less congestion and pollution, and the social services are not overstretched.

3) Community services might be under-used, e.g., in the declining regions, schools are often not fully utilised.

4) Unemployment in some regions causes a migration of the younger more enterprising members of the community , resulting in further regional depression.

5) For maximum economic growth, all resources should be fully utilised, i.e., all regions in the country (and not just certain regions in the country) should be developed.

6) If certain regions continue to have high levels of unemployment, the heavy government expenditure on welfare services would be a burden on the tax-payer.

7) All the above-mentioned government policies might have strong political implications.

38. LABOUR

1) The labour force or work-force constitutes the human resources that are available for economic activity.

2) The following are the factors which determine the size of the labour force:-

i) Total size of the population.

ii) Minimum statutory school-leaving age.

iii) Number of people who are in full-time education above the age of 16.

iv) Retirement age.

v) Number of people who work beyond the retirement age, which might be affected by the level of retirement pension available and by the earning rules for pensioners.

vi) Number of working housewives, which is affected by the changes in general attitudes to working wives and mothers and by the attempts to gain higher standards of living.

vii) Level of available social security benefits (certain earnings related to social security benefits might deter people from working).

viii) Number of hours worked and number of holidays taken in the year would significantly determine the annual supply of labour in the economy.

3) The following are the factors which determine the efficiency of the labour force:-

i) Equipment (capital) used by the labour force.

ii) Level of education of the work-force. (Workers have to have a high level training to maximise efficiency as technology becomes more complex.)

iii) Efficiency of the organisation. (Is the company making the best use of human resources?)

iv) Industrial relations/management attitudes - good relations between management and union ensure industrial peace (minimise strikes) and allow higher productivity and technological changes to take place.

v) Industrial relations/union attitudes - whether to accept redundancies caused by the adoption of modern technology or to resist technological change (extent to which demarcation is enforced).

vi) Health of the labour force.

vii) Age pattern of the labour force.

viii) Working conditions, e.g., efficient lighting, ventilation and other environmental factors, which could help to improve productivity.

4) Occupational mobility is the ability of workers to move from one occupation to another.

5) As the speed of technological change increases and some industries need to expand while others decline, occupational mobility is becoming increasingly important.

6) The following are barriers to occupational mobility:-
   i) Natural abilities, e.g., intelligence, physical strength and stamina.
   ii) Period of training - matured men and women would find it very difficult to under go a lengthy period of training without great financial assistance.
   iii) Lack of financial incentive - the wage or salary is too low to make the occupational change worthwhile.
   iv) Age - potential employers would not be willing to train workers who are approaching the retirement age.
   v) Trade unions - where there is a "closed shop" policya worker could not be employed without a union card which is not readily given.
   vi) Personal reasons - preference for remaining unemployed and waiting for an opening in last occupation rather than change jobs, the alternative occupations might be considered undesirable (e.g., unattractive working conditions), ignorance of the vacancies in other industries or of the qualifications required or training available, etc..

7) Occupational mobility could be improved in the following ways:-
   i) Retraining programs organised by the government, with assistance given to workers who undertake them.
   ii) Provision of more information, e.g., through local job-centres and government advertising.

8) Geographical mobility refers to the willingness or ability of workers to move about the country in search of jobs, the employment opportunities varying from region to region.

9) The following are the barriers to geographical mobility:-
   i) Family reasons, e.g., loss of friends, dependent relatives, problems associated with changing schools or the jobs of the other working members in the family, etc..
   ii) Expenses - the costs of buying and selling a house and removal expenses.
   iii) Accommodation - those who do not own a house have to rent one, which might not be readily available.
   iv) Prejudice - though employment opportunities exist in many industrialised areas, these industrialised areas are considered to live in because of congestion and pollution.
   v) Ignorance or lack of knowledge of the employment opportunities in other parts of the country.
   vi) Lack of financial incentive - there is sometimes no incentive to look for work in other parts of the country because of the levels of unemployment, social security benefits and tax rates on wages.

10) Geographical mobility could be increased in the following ways:-

    i)   Local or central government grants as subsidies for removal expenses.

    ii)   Provision of hostel and other accommodation.

    iii)   Provision of travel warrants for workers who are separated from their families.

    iv)   Circulation of information pertaining to job opportunities.

11) The labour force could be distributed amongst the following sectors in the economy:-

    i)   Primary sector.

    ii)   Secondary sector.

    iii)   Tertiary sector.

    iv)   Quaternary sector. (This sector has evolved in recent years, based on the revolution in IT, and includes IT support services, internet services and computer technology upgrading services.)

39. WAGES AND UNIONS

1) In a planned economy, the state determines the level of wages paid to workers.

2) In a free enterprise economy, the wage (price) level for labour, as it does for all other goods, is determined by the market forces of supply and demand.

Wages

1) In Britain, wages are partly determined by the market forces of supply and demand, and partly by the policy of the government and attitudes of the trade unions.

2) The following are factors which govern the supply of labour for a particular occupation:-

    i)   The size of the labour force/population - af fected by births and deaths, immigration and emigration, and, legislation determining the school-leaving and retirement ages.

    ii)   The degree of natural skill and ability required, e.g., the special skills of the brain sur geon would always be in short supply while the minimal skills of a shop assistant would be readily available.

    iii)   The length of training required, e.g., doctors, solicitors and pilots require relatively long periods of training.

    iv)   The attractiveness of the job, e.g., "glamour" jobs such as airline pilots and professional footballers are potentially high in supply while jobs such as refuse collectors and miners are potentially low in supply.

3) The following are factors governing the demand for labour in a particular occupation:-

   i) Labour is a derived demand - the demand for a product caused by changes in fashions or a successful advertising campaign would affect the demand for labour to produce that product.

   ii) In a free enterprise economy, firms engage labour to produce goods and services and sell them for a profit - labour would be employed up to the point where the value of the last man's output equals his cost (wages) to the firm, a concept that is known as the mar ginal productivity theory of wages.

   iii) The possibility of replacing labour with capital, e.g., machines, for instance, when increases in wages make labour more expensive than machinery, causing the demand for labour to fall.

   iv) Certain industries are labour-intensive, whereby machines are unable to replace labour, e.g., the hospitality and health-care industries.

Trade Unions

1) Trade unions affect the supply of labour in the following ways:-

   i) By obtaining and enforcing a closed shop policy , whereby all employees performing certain jobs have to be members of a particular trade union.

   ii) By having a sufficiently large proportion of union members in the work-force, whereby acting together makes it possible for them to exercise power in negotiations with employers.

2) The following are the effects of trade unions on the supply of labour:-

   i) Maintaining an increase, or preventing a decrease, in the number of jobs for union members by insisting on agreed manning levels.

   ii) Strengthening the bar gaining position of workers in wage negotiations by threatening or carrying out industrial action, e.g., strikes, go-slow, overtime ban, withdrawal of "goodwill", working-to-rule, etc..

3) Due to trade union pressure, wages in some industries are higher than free market forces would indicate.

4) The following are the types of unions:-

   i) Craft unions (restricted to skilled workers)

   ii) Industrial unions (open to all skilled and unskilled workers in one industry)

   iii) General unions (open to skilled and unskilled workers in dif ferent trades and industries)

iv)   White collar unions (restricted to non-manual workers, e.g., bank clerks, teachers and civil servants)

5)   Most trade unions are organised as follows:-

   i)   Plant and factory level (represented by an unpaid shop steward who negotiates at factory level with management)

   ii)   Local units or branch level (represented by elected regional and national delegates who deal with local issues)

   iii) Union conferences elect national executive and formulate national policy

   iv)   National Executive, normally dominated by the General Secretary, implements union policy throughout the year

6) The unions could carry out any of the following industrial action:-

   i)   Official strike (called by the union executive)

   ii)   Unofficial strike (called at the factory level usually by the shop steward(s) without executive approval)

   iii) Work-to-rule (involves a ban on overtime, with employees working in accordance with strict procedures)

   iv)   Closed shop (only union members are allowed to work in the firm concerned)

   v)   Picketing (involves some workers trying to persuade other workers not to enter a firm to work during a strike period)

Employers' Federations/Associations

1)   Employers' federations/associations represent the major firms in an industry.

2)   They represent the employers' side in collective bargaining with unions to determine a basic national wage rate.

3)   They also provide a range of services such as providing advice on modern developments in industry and on problems of redundancy , and, taking part in negotiations with the government and other bodies.

Government Policy

1)   Governments have increasingly attempted to influence the level of wage increases since the early 1960s.

2)   Strong persuasive methods and incomes policies in various forms have been used, and have been often applied to all industries and all workers, completely ignoring the varying conditions of demand and supply of labour in certain industries.

Factors Determining Wage Levels

1)   Proportion of labour cost to total costs - where labour costs are relatively

low employers would often accede to wage demands to avoid lost production.

2) Elasticity of demand for a product - wage demands would be more readily acceded to if increased costs could be passed on to customers in higher prices without a significant fall in demand.

3) Profit record of industries - industries which make high profits are likely to be pressured to give wage increases.

4) Essential nature of industry - in industries which are crucial to the economy such as water, gas and electricity, industrial action could influence public opinion to push employers to give in to wage demands.

5) Strength of trade unions - well organised unions with a large number of members in the work-force could easily press for and obtain high pay for workers.

6) Social justice - public opinion might urge the government to increase certain wages, e.g., the wages of nurses.

7) Differentials - a differential is the difference between the wages of one group of workers and another, e.g., workers in the same industry fall into the broad groups of skilled, semi-skilled and unskilled, wherein the demands for wage increases for one group are based on what has happened to another group, regardless of economic circumstances, for instance, a ten per cent wage increase for skilled workers because of increased productivity might lead to a demand for ten per cent wage increase for unskilled workers whose productivity does not match that of the skilled workers.

Other Aspects Of Wages

1) Real wages and money (nominal) wages - money wage is the wage expressed in terms of amounts of money while real wage is the amount of goods and services which could be purchased with the money wage.

2) Economic rent is income received over and above that which is necessary to keep a factor of production (usually labour) in its present us; it is payment for special talents or abilities which are in short supply relative to the demand for them; it is the difference between what a worker gets and the least he would be prepared to accept, i.e., the extra amount above the least he would be prepared to accept. The least the worker would be prepared to accept is known as transfer earning.

3) Wage drift is the difference between the gross earnings (which include commission, allowances, incentives, etc.) and the agreed minimum wage.

4) Piece rate relates payment to output or productivity, e.g., $10.00 per finished garment, while time rate involves payment for every hour worked, e.g., $5.00 per hour.

5) The advantages of piece rate are as follows:-
   i) It is an incentive to greater effort and rewards efficiency.
   ii) Workers do not have to be strictly supervised as it is in their own interests to produce the maximum output.
   iii) As labour costs per unit of output is known, costs of production could be easily calculated.
   iv) Boredom is a major problem in many occupations, but piece rate presents a challenge to the worker in that he would strive for a high output so that he could get high rewards.

6) The following are the problems of applying piece rate:-
   i) Maximum output is not always needed as the demand might fall.
   ii) It is not always possible to measure the output per worker.
   iii) Disputes might arise regarding how much should be paid for each article produced.
   iv) As speed becomes the workers' main concern, quality is likely to deteriorate, and, a system of quality control should be in place.
   v) Any delays in the production process could result in industrial unrest.
   vi) Workers might demand expensive equipment which is not always carefully maintained.

7) In view of the above problems for applying piece rate, it might be more feasible to have some form of time rate.

8) Gross wages and net wages - the gross wage is the amount earned by a worker before stoppages such as income tax and national insurance contributions while the net wage (take-home pay) is the amount earned after these stoppages.

40. ENTREPRENEURSHIP

Why Do People Set Up In Business?

1) The desire for financial wealth.
2) To fulfill a dream - to realise an ambition, e.g., to set up a business empire for future generations.
3) To redistribute wealth - from the rich to the poor.e.g., from the first world to the third world.
4) To provide a service to customers - to see that the customer is satisfied with your company's product or service and is happy , especially after having experienced poor customer service or poor quality products yourself.

5) To have an interesting job - to avoid working in a dead-end, routine, boring job under an employer.

6) To have freedom of action - to avoid working under an unpleasant, autocratic boss, and to have the all-embracing challenge of a business - to be involved in all the aspects of a business, e.g., production, marketing, personnel and finance.

7) To fund an ambition or personal goal - wealth gained from the business might be used to fund a hobby or an important project, e.g., for the needy and the poor.

Is Profit A Dirty Word?

1) Business survival depends on financial stability.

2) Financial stability depends on:
   i) profit, which enables the business to grow
   ii) available cash, which allows business transactions to be carried out, e.g., with customers and suppliers

3) A business needs to make a profit to gain access to other funds, e.g., a bank loan, to fund its growth. A profit-making company is more likely to be able to get a loan from a bank than a company making losses.

4) A profit-making company could reward its owners (investors) for taking the risk of investing in it. Potential investors would find it more attractive to invest in a profit-making company . A profit-making company is therefore more able to obtain funds for expansion than a loss-making company.

How Are Businesses Born?

1) A business normally begins with an idea, e.g., a business providing window cleaning services.

2) The driving force of a business has to come from an entrepreneur , the person who undertakes the risk of investing in the business.

3) A business might also be the result of an invention, e.g., a new design for a vacuum cleaner.

4) Careful planning is required for starting a business, i.e., a business plan stating the various stages and objectives of the business should be drawn up.

5) The business plan guides the business owner(s) so that it is possible to continually monitor and review progress.

6) The business plan could also be used to persuade other providers of capital to finance the business both as it is starting up (seed capital) and as it is growing (development capital).

The Business Plan

1) The business plan states the details of a business, e.g., the marketing, financial and operational aspects of the business.

2) A typical business plan would have the following:-

   i) Details of the business - name, location, physical size, etc..

   ii) Goals and objectives - Mention the general (mission) statement of the business at the beginning with regards to what it actually wants to achieve, e.g., providing quality service to customers and meaningful, challenging work to employees. State the objectives of the business, e.g., achieving a market share of 40% in the second year of operation, operating within the budget or breaking even within the first 18 months of business.

   iii) Present state of the market - in terms of the sales volume or revenue, location of the market and prospects for further growth.

   iv) Customer profile - State the characteristics of targeted customers, e.g., their income levels, sex, location, etc..

   v) Competition analysis:

      a) Carry out a detailed analysis of competitors' products and their strengths, so that the business could have a better product than the competitors' in terms of functions and features.

      b) Compare the price with the prices of competitors, devise a pricing policy and forecast sales volume and break-even point.

      c) Plan the methods and estimate the costs of promotion and advertising.

   vi) Projection of sales volume and revenue in the short and long term. Make sales forecasts based on the objectives of the business and certain assumptions, e.g., the assumption that competitors would not reduce their prices to capture a bigger share of the market.

   vii) Present orders - A new business would be able to obtain loans from banks more easily if there is evidence of (new) orders.

   viii) Assets and required financing - New machinery, new suppliers of raw materials and possibly storage space would be needed for any business expansion. They would require finance.

   ix) Staff - the capabilities, backgrounds and ambitions of the staff and the number of new staff needed in the near future.

   x) External factors - the bank interest rates, the availability of labour, etc..

   xi) Ownership - who the owners of the business are, their percentage share in the business, the actual amount they have invested in the business and the expected profits for the owners.

xii) Financial forecast - This would include a projection of profit and cash flow, so that the business would know the periods when extra finance might be needed and the bank might be approached for loans.

What Are The Typical Problems A New Business Faces?

1) The setting up of a business might look great, but running a business takes up a lot of time, e.g., working seven days a week to get it going.

2) The likelihood of business failure happening during the first one or two years is much higher than later.

3) Failure in the first two years tends to be the result of:-

   i) Lack of market research -What is regarded as an interesting idea by the businessman might not appeal at all to the mass market, e.g., wonderful new gadgets invented by engineers might not be in great demand.

   ii) Insignificance in the market-place - Small companies lack respectability, and, the lar ger customers might pay them late, knowing that the small businesses could not afford to sue them.

   iii) Cash flow problems - The small business, because they purchase little, might not obtain long periods of credit or discounts from suppliers.

   iv) Lack of skill - The entrepreneur might lack the technical skill, personal drive and ambition to operate the business.

   v) Lack of finance - This is one of the most common reasons why business fail. If the business has been making losses for some time, e.g., two years, the bank or other financiers would probably not want to make loans to the business and the business would be forced into liquidation.

   vi) Over-expansion (overtrading) - A business, especially a smaller business, might expand too quickly , spending a lot of money on more machines, more materials and more labour , and might encounter cash-flow problems if they spent more than they received from customers.

   vii) Megalomania - One business success could make the owners feel that whatever they produce would result in a successful venture, e.g., Sir Clive Sinclair gained his initial and formidable success as the man who anticipated the demand for a pocket calculator later had some weird and wonderful ideas, e.g., the Sinclair C5, the demand for which was not researched, which became one of the most famous failures in corporate history.

What Are The Conditions For Business Success?

1) Probably, the best way to find an answer to this is to ask the various successful business people.

2) Successful business people would probably give some of the following reasons for their success:-

   i) A well designed product. A business should carry out a careful and thoughtful market research to discover the customer needs. They have to produce an exciting and interesting product which fulfills a particular need or want, which customers are willing or able to pay for.

   ii) Imagination. The creation of certain products would need a highly imaginative mind, e.g., a bank without any branches (First Direct), internet shopping and taking cash from automated telling machines (ATMs).

   iii) Tight financial control. A budget should be formulated and then communicated to the rest of the business as something which has to be adhered to very closely. A business focused on profit and cash flow is most likely to generate financial wealth for survival and then growth. But sometimes it is necessary for the business to borrow from the bank.

   iv) Motivated employees and directors. There should be motivated employees and directors who are willing to work hard for the success of the business and themselves.

   v) An efficient production system. There should be highly skilled people with initiative to run an efficient and flexible production system.

   vi) Commitment and vision. For success in business, commitment and vision are needed, as in, e.g., the case of James Dyson, who invented the revolutionary bagless vacuum cleaner.

41. ORGANISATION OF ECONOMIC ACTIVITIES

1) Businesses are either part of the private sector or the public sector.

2) The business is part of the private sector if it is owned by firms and individuals.

3) It is in the public sector if it is owned by the government (or the state).

4) A few businesses, e.g., the British Nuclear Fuels Limited, are owned by the government, but are run on a private sector, profit-making basis.

Private Sector

1) Unincorporated Companies

   i) The unincorporated business is not a separate legal entityThe owner and the business are one and the same person in the eyes of the law who would be sued or fined for any wrongdoing.

ii) The owner of the unincorporated business has unlimited liability , i.e., there is no limit on the amount of assets, e.g., the owner's house, etc., which could be sold off to meet the debts of the business, if the unincorporated business is sued or goes into liquidation.

iii) An unincorporated company could be either of the following:

   a) A sole proprietor or trader

   b) A partnership

Sole Traders (Sole Proprietorships)

1) The sole trader has total ownership of and responsibility for managing the business.

2) The sole proprietorship is the most common form of business and is how most businesses start their life.

3) In order to start as a sole trader , only a few procedures have to be undertaken.

4) After registering the name of the business (with Companies House in Cardiff, U.K.), the sole trader is free to start trading.

5) Checks would be made during registration to ensure that the name of the business is original.

6) It does not require much capital to be a sole trader who often relies on his own savings or a bank loan to finance the business.

7) As a sole proprietorship is easy to set up, there are many sole traders.

8) The sole trader often rents the office, which eliminates the need to find large sums of money.

9) Members of the family, who are perhaps not as expensive as employing staff, often work in the sole proprietorship.

10) The advantages and disadvantages of the sole proprietorship are as follows:-

Advantages

i) The profit belongs to the owner.

ii) The sole trader exercises total control over the business.

iii) There is a lot of variety in the sole trader 's work as he has to do practically everything, e.g., buying, selling, delivery accounts, etc..

iv) It is highly motivating to work for oneself.

Disadvantages

i) The sole trader has to do everything and may not have enough finance to engage additional help.

ii) The sole trader works long hours as he does not have enough funds to employ specialist staff.

iii)   He has unlimited liability.

iv)   He has difficulty competing with the larger companies.

v)   He has no one to share the risks with, who could hold discussions with him.

Partnerships

1)   The Partnership Act of 1890 gives the legal definition of a partnership.

2)   A partnership comprises of two or more people operating a business for the common goal of making a profit.

3)   The partners share the responsibility for running the business and any profit that might be generated by the business.

4)   Most partnerships are small businesses, often in retailing, building, or the professional services, e.g., accountants, doctors and solicitors.

5)   Up to 20 partners are permitted in any one partnership (with a few exceptions for some professional partnerships).

6)   With more people involved in running the business, the partners could specialise, where possible. For example, a law firm might have several partners, with one specialising in litigation (court work), another in probate (wills), another in conveyancing (buying and selling of property) and another in possibly the most lucrative area, commercial law (company business).

7)   There are few legalities for setting up a partnership, though there are several rights related to this kind of business. (These rights are laid out in a Deed of Partnership which could be verbal or in writing.)

8)   The Deed of Partnership would include the following details on the roles of the partners:-

i)   Whether the partners are "active" or actually running the business or "sleeping" partners, i.e., contribute finance to the business but do not involve in the actual running of the business.

ii)   The amount of capital (money) each would invest in the business.

iii) How any profit is to be shared.

iv)   How the partnership could be terminated.

v)   How the partnership could be expanded (taking on more partners).

vi)   Whether a partner could have limited liability (although at least one partner must have unlimited liability).

vii) The dissolution of the partnership if one partner dies. Should a partner die, it is usual for the existing partners to re-form immediately using the same format for the Deed of Partnership.

9) The advantages and disadvantages of the partnership are as follows:-

Advantages

i) As there are no formalities to comply with, a partnership is cheap to set up.

ii) Specialisation of job functions by the partners allows for greater efficiency and therefore lower costs.

iii) The partners could share the burden of the work.

iv) With more owners, the potential for obtaining more finance is greater

v) As the partners could share their knowledge and expertise, they could make better decisions.

Disadvantages

i) Each partner has less control of the business, as each has to share the decision-making.

ii) Each partner has to share the burden of the poor decisions or work of the other partners.

iii) There might be arguments among the partners and decisions might take longer to be made.

iv) Whether the partners work hard or not, any profits are shared.

v) There is unlimited liability.

vi) Finance is restricted to 20 partners.

vii) On the death of a partner, continuity might be broken.

Unlimited Liability And Incorporation

1) As the sole proprietorship and the partnership are unincorporated, they face the major problem of unlimited liability.

2) To overcome this problem of unlimited liability and to allow for greater expansion by gaining greater access to finance, the business should become incorporated.

Incorporation

1) A company which has its own separate legal entity is known as an incorporated company.

2) An incorporated company could enter into contracts, make legal claims and face legal claims that are made against it in the name of the business and not in the name of the owners of the business.

3) An incorporated company has to submit documents to the Registrar of Joint Stock Companies before a Certificate of Incorporation is issued.

4) The documents to be submitted are the Memorandum ofAssociation and the Articles of Association.

5) Memorandum of Association - Under the Companies Act of 1985, the

details related to the purpose of the company have to be included in this document. The other important elements are: name, location of registered office, limited liability, nominal capital and whether the company is public limited.

6) Articles of Association - The internal rules for the operation of the company are to be included in this document.The other details to be included are: the rights of the shareholders, the frequency of company meetings and the responsibilities of the directors.

Limited Liability

1) The owners of an incorporated company could be liable only for the amount of money that they have invested in it.

2) If the incorporated company is liquidated, the assets of the owners could not be used to cover the debts of the business.

3) Limited companies are often family owned businesses which have grown from either sole proprietorships or partnerships which required more finance in order to achieve growth.

4) The limited liability ensures that the owners of the business have less risks whilst allowing some control of the business to be maintained. Should the company close down due to losses, the owners or shareholders of the business only lose the amount of money they have invested in the company

5) The shareholders or owners of limited companies take a proportion or share of any profit made.

6) All the shareholders could select the directors and chairperson at the annual general meeting (AGM) of the business.

7) There are two types of limited company, viz., private limited companies and public limited companies.

Private Limited Companies (Ltd)

1) Under the Companies Act of 1980, limited companies have to have at least two members or shareholders though there is no upper limit.

2) Also, the word "limited" has to appear in the name of the company. This is to allow other businesses to know the type of company they are trading with.

3) Shares in the private limited companies might only be sold privatelyThey are not allowed to be bought and sold by members of the general public.

4) The following are the advantages and disadvantages of private limited companies:-

Advantages

i) As there is no limit to the number of shareholders, access to capital is better than for unincorporated companies.

ii) The limited liability of the incorporated company makes investing in it less risky, which in turn attracts more investors.

iii) As the shares are sold privately, some control over the business is possible.

iv) Should a shareholder die, the business could still continue (the deceased's shares could be sold to another by invitation).

Disadvantages

i) The legal documentation required for the formation of the business is time consuming and expensive.

ii) The company's financial accounts have to be filed with the Registrar of Companies and they could be viewed by members of the public, including competitors.

iii) Shares cannot be sold to the general public. This means it is harder to raise capital.

iv) Profits have to be shared and have to be distributed to the shareholders.

Public Limited Companies (PLC)

1) There are fewer PLCs than limited companies.

2) PLCs are larger than the limited companies.

3) Similar to the private limited companies, there has to be a minimum of two shareholders.

4) A company "going public" has to complete the following procedures:-

i) Issue a prospectus.

ii) Make an announcement of the intention to "go public" to enable any member of the public to have the opportunity to invest in the company.

iii) After the company is "floated", the shares of the company might be bought and sold by members of the public, pension fund managers, insurance companies, etc..

iv) Owners of ordinary shares could vote (one vote per share owned) at the compulsory AGM where directors are selected or rejected.

5) In Britain, quite a number of soccer clubs have gone public, which is probably a quick way to obtain additional finance.

6) A spate of building societies have also changed from being a friendly society or mutualised company to a PLC, not just for additional finance but as a way of competing with other similar financial institutions (friendly societies are owned by their members or customers, each having a vote irrespective of the amount of money invested).

7) PLCs represent the largest proportion of our economic activity.

8) The advantages and disadvantages of going public are as follows:-
Advantages

i) There is access to a much greater source of finance in the present, i.e., going public allows the company to invite anyone to buy shares (a new issue) and thus it is not restricting the ownership.

ii) There is also access to much finance in the future. The company could either issue shares to present shareholders (known as a rights issue) or it could issue more shares to the open market (another new issue). A rights issue would be cheaper as the company would be sending an offer to purchase the shares to the present shareholders. Thus, it would not have to spend so much money on marketing the share issue.

iii) Being a public listed company is a prestigeThough customers might not be impressed by the public listing, suppliers, especially the smaller companies, would be likely to benefit from having a public listed company as a customer , e.g., as a reference for marketing purposes.

iv) There is access to other forms of financeThe larger size and greater stability of the public listed company make it easier to obtain bank loans and possibly at lower rates of interest as well.

v) There is a reduction in gearing. Gearing measures the ratio of borrowed money to the amount of money raised through shares. This means that borrowing money from a bank, which is more expensive, is reduced.

Disadvantages

i) It is costly launching the business on the stock market, e.g., a prospectus would have to be printed and a merchant bank is normally hired as the underwriters as protection against the share issue failing to attract enough investment.

ii) The issuing of shares means that the business has more shareholders to manage and communicate with. This necessitates the costs incurred for the printing of interim reports (the interim report charts the progress of the business during the first six months of the year) and annual reports (the annual report is issued at the end of the year and is a much more detailed account of the yearwith a report by the directors, a full set of financial statements and details of future plans). This is to promote the image of the or ganisation, so that it would easily attract investors and the share price would be buoyant.

iii) Dividends are paid on each share for as long as the share is owned and in the hands of the shareholderWhenever new shares are issued, total dividends have to increase to meet the dividends requirement on the extra shares. This could be far more onerous than the benefit of extra funds.

iv) A family business going public would bring in outside ownership. This might reduce the amount of influence the family has over decision-making, though the family might try to ensure that its shareholding is more than 50%. This might mean that the business is unable to raise as much funds as it otherwise could. Unless the business uses a rights issue to raise more money each shareholder's percentage of ownership might fall as more shares are issued.

v) There is the threat of takeover by a predator company The predator company could buy up the shares and put in a takeover bid if the share price of the company falls. Even if the share price of the company were rising, a predator company with a great deal of surplus cash might buy up the shares and take over the company if it thinks that by owning the company it would add much more value to the wealth of its own company , compared with the cost of the tar get business.

Public Sector

1) The public sector comprises of businesses owned by or accountable to the government (either central or local government).

2) Most of the capital required to operate public sector businesses is obtained by the government through taxation revenue.

3) All public sector companies are public corporations which have incorporated status, like private sector businesses.

4) Public sector companies have their own legal status and therefore could enter into contracts or be sued, like any other incorporated company.

5) Public corporations in Britain include the nationalised industries, which have been privatised by Mar garet Thatcher's governments from 1979 onwards, e.g., the utilities such as gas, electricity and water.

6) The Bank of England and the BBC are also public corporations which are accountable to certain government departments.

7) The BBC gets a "grant" from the government in the form of TV licence money.

8) Government departments are also responsible for various "businesses". For example, the Department of Health takes responsibility for running the National Health Service.

Privatisation

1) Privatisation is the process of transferring the ownership of public sector bodies to the private sector.

2) In Britain, Mar garet Thatcher's Conservative government had

implemented a series of privatisations partly on political grounds, as mentioned earlier.

3) Privatisation involved selling government businesses and deregulating certain sectors, e.g., the bus and coach industry , to allow companies to bid for the right to operate certain routes, exposing most of these businesses to market forces.

4) Privatisation would encourage efficiency and provide an important source of finance for the government. For example, the sale of British Gas in 1986 raised about £6.5 billion.

5) Many other companies were also privatised in Britain, besides British Gas.

6) Barriers to entry into the various markets which had been in place to protect the nationalised industries from competition were removed to ensure that the privatisation process ran smoothly.

7) The following are the advantages and disadvantages of privatisation:-

Advantages

i) The business is likely to be more efficient.

ii) The government expenditure in the form of subsidies is saved.

iii) Efficiency might lead to lower costs which could be passed on to the consumer or greater profits which are passed to shareholders.

iv) Members of the public have the opportunity to become shareholders in major British companies (part of the ownership culture).

Disadvantages

i) Selling the business away results in lost revenue opportunities, e.g., before privatisation BT was a profit-making business.

ii) Selling off public corporations might be viewed as the sale of what belongs to the general public.

iii) The improved efficiency of the business after privatising would be likely to lead to a reduction in the number of employees, therefore increasing unemployment.

iv) The privatising of the utilities such as gas, electricity and water means that the government would not be able to influence the prices of many products within the economy . All firms have to have fuel, heat and light, phones and transport. Any change in the price of these affects costs and consequently the prices of other goodsAfter privatisation, most of these costs fell.

Local Authority

1) The authorities are an important but often for gotten example of public sector business.

2) They provide a broad range of services such as education, housing and social services in the community.

3) They are often one of the largest employers in any given area.

4) The finance for their services comes from the central government (which is responsible for nearly half of the revenue), the council tax (which is set and collected by the authority), loans and the revenue from the provision of local amenities such as swimming pools and leisure centres, the latter accounting only for a very small percentage of income.

5) The elected local councillors who make up the local council are responsible for administering the services and collecting the revenues.

42. MERGERS AND ACQUISITIONS

What Are Mergers, Takeovers And Acquisitions?

1) A merger is the voluntary joining together of two or more firms to form one business in order to improve their profitabilityproductivity or market position.

2) A takeover is the gaining control of a business by another business. A takeover is considered "hostile" if a controlling interest is bought without the consent or blessing of the management of the business which is being taken over.

3) An acquisition is the gaining control of part of a business by another business. One of a company's businesses might be sold off if there is no desire to keep it or if it no longer fits into its future objectives.

Why Do Businesses Join Together?

1) In most cases, costs reduction is the reason.

2) A combined business could result in savings due to the increase in its size.

3) Growing in size could be achieved quickly through a meger, takeover or acquisition.

4) A company could sometimes grow because of the incredible success of its products, e.g., Microsoft.

5) One of the main reasons why companies join together is to benefit from economies of scale.

Economies Of Scale

1) Businesses joining together could result in huge savings in marketing, production and research and development. For example, BP's takeover of Amoco in the U.K. has helped to reduce costs, as profit margins have been falling due to the fall in the price of crude oil.

2) By joining together, the combined business is able to spread the cost of

many activities, which results in a reduction of the unit cost. For example, spending £1,000 million on research and development (R & D) for a new car for the company planning to sell 100,000 cars means that the unit cost for R & D would be £1,000. After the merger or joining together, a similar venture with a now increased sales figure of 150,000 cars would reduce the unit cost to £667.

3)   This reduction in costs results in a competitive price for the combined business's product.

4)   Companies joining together or mer ging would have assets with higher value. Because of this, financial institutions are more willing to provide finance to the merged companies. The cost of a bank loan thus obtained in terms of the interests to be paid, would be spread over more products, therefore reducing the cost per unit. In addition, the bank might favour the now larger combined business with a lower interest rate.

5)   Bulk buying could now be achieved, resulting in a reduction of the cost of purchasing raw materials.

Types Of Integration

A benefit of companies joining together or merging is integration.

Horizontal Integration

1)   Horizontal integration is the mer ger of two companies which are in the same stage of production. For example, two companies producing garden furniture are both involved in the secondary stage of production and are producing the same product.

2)   Horizontal integration results in economies of scale, e.g., purchasing and technical economies.

3)   Standardisation of parts might be possible.

4)   The combined company might be able to have a greater influence in the market or be more competitive.

5)   The combined company would be less likely to be the victim of a takeover

Vertical Integration

1)   Vertical integration is the joining together of two companies from diferent stages of production. For example, a garden furniture manufacturer joins together with a timber merchant, resulting in the garden furniture manufacturer having a reliable supply of wood, which could be purchased at cost, to produce the furniture, resulting in increased profits.

2)   Vertical integration between a manufacturer and a retailer provides the manufacturer with a ready-made outlet for its products. This results in a decrease in marketing cost.

3) There are two types of vertical integration, which are as follows:-

    i)   Backward Vertical Integration

        A company joins with another from an earlier stage of production, e.g., a retailer mer ging with a manufacturer or a manufacturer merging with a supplier of raw materials.

    ii)   Forward Vertical Integration

        A company involved in the extraction of a raw material joins with a manufacturer.

4) There are a few companies which are perfectly integrated, i.e., they own companies with each stage of production and therefore have complete control of the whole process of distribution of their products from the extraction of the raw materials to the retail outlets. Shell, e.g., has its own oilfields, tankers to transfer the crude oil to its own refineries and its own petrol stations.

Conglomerate Integration

1) Conglomerate integration is the joining together of two unrelated companies, regardless of the stage of production they are involved in.

2) An important reason for such companies joining together is diversification. Joining together would give the company a portfolio of products and not just a range of products, thus reducing risks.

3) The lar ger company or owner or parent company within the group of companies is the holding company. The holding company is responsible for the objectives and long-term policy of the group of companies but allows them to operate as separate entities.

4) Conglomerate integration reduces the reliance on one type of product and thus reduces the risk of being badly affected by a downturn in a given market.

5) The companies within the group could share many overheads, thus reducing costs.

6) Conglomerate integration is popular amongst retail outlets as it allows the outlets to sell a wide range of products under one roof.

7) The majority of the companies under the group or conglomerate might have no obvious connection at all. For example, Granada is the owner of Granada TV, Yorkshire TV and LWT, Little Chef, Travelodge, Meridian hotels and Posthouse hotels and has just purchased a ten per cent stake in Liverpool Football Club.

Globalisation And Access To New Markets

1) The increased growth of multinational companies is due to the attempt of businesses to take advantage of the resultant economies of scale and the access to the different markets around the world.

2) Companies have to be large enough to cope with the stiff competition in the international market. They could buy over other companies or merge with other companies. They could either buy or be bought! For example, Kingfisher has been negotiating a mer ger with Asda and having talks with German DIY businesses, and, Zeneca has been trying to mege with Swedish drug company Astra.

Asset Stripping

Some holding companies or conglomerates acquire other companies in order to sell off the parts that would yield a profit. This process is known as asset stripping.

Survival

1) A company which is short of cash or afraid of being unable to compete with larger rivals could resort to merging or being taken over in order to enhance the chances of survival.

2) For example, a company would invite another company to bid for it to avoid being acquired by another company also bidding for it, as the company suspects that the latter company would act as an asset stripper and thereby sell off its main brands at a great profit.

Synergy

1) By merging, the combined business would be more ef ficient and more able to dominate the market than the two separate businesses before the merger. (Synergy means: 2 + 2 = 5)

2) It is often quicker to purchase brands owned by another company , as building a brand takes a long time and is carried out at great expense.

3) It might be desirable to purchase the entire company which makes the brands when the individual brands are not for sale.

4) Acquiring another company might be costly but this could be more than offset by the profit brought in by the acquired company.

Access To New Technology

1) A company acquiring another company with a new technology would save on having to spend much money on research and purchasing new machinery.

2) Mergers and takeovers appear to increase and decrease in numbers in a cyclical manner. It appears that when the economy is booming and businesses are growing there are more mergers and takeovers, and, when there is a recession the number of mergers and takeovers decreases.

3) Governments might actively encourage mergers in an attempt to improve international competitiveness and chances of survival in overseas markets.

4) Many shareholders, especially the bigger shareholders such as pension

funds and other financial institutions, are in favour of a takeover because of the short-term gain, e.g., high share prices and dividends, rather than because of any improvements in the long-term prospects of the company

Demergers

1) There could be problems with increases in business size such as the problems of organising and communicating within a lage enterprise, and, control.

2) There could be diseconomies of scale, which would lead to an increase in the average cost of goods. The increase in unit costs might mean that the company's prices are uncompetitive, resulting in a decline in sales.

3) This means that the company would not be able to enjoy the benefits of economies of scale such as buying in bulk, thus making it even less competitive.

4) Alternatively, if the company absorbs the increase in costs as a result of the diseconomies, it might lead to a drop in profits which could dissatisfy the shareholders.

5) Either scenario could lead to a demer ger or breaking up of the mer ged business.

6) For example, BAT got rid of its financial services sector and Nabisco, the cereal giant, disposed of RJR, which has been the producer of Camel cigarettes and Oreo cookies.

43. SIZES OF BUSINESS UNITS

Different Measures Of Size

The following are some methods of measuring business size:-

1) Revenue - The value of products sold

   i) Revenue could be used to measure the size of any business. It is frequently used for comparing lage businesses, e.g., food retailers, Safeway and Asda, frequently quote revenue and market share to demonstrate their size and influence in the market-place.

   ii) Market growth, which is related to revenue, is also frequently used, especially for forecasting the future size of the business.

2) Capital employed - The amount of money tied up in (net) assets by shareholders

   i) This could be found by studying sets of company reports.

   ii) It is more appropriate for manufacturing companies or companies which deal in property (either developing it or letting it to other companies). This is because, unlike the service industry , much of the manufacturing companies' or property developers' capital are tied up in fixed assets.

  iii) The other measurement of size is based on the amount of cash the company holds, e.g., Nomura Securities was once rumoured to be able to buy the four major high street banks in Britain with petty cash.

3) Volume

  i) The volume of production in a company could be used as a measure of its size.

  ii) However, others such as the marketing manager might be concerned about the value of the production as well.

4) Profit

  i) The measurement of a company's size based on its profit is rather crude.

  ii) Due to differences in accounting regulations, it is very difficult to make international comparisons.

  iii) The profit should be viewed in relation to revenue.

  iv) Profit alone might not be a reliable measure of size because of the subjective methods of measuring profit.

  v) The main reason for using profit is to evaluate how much the business might be worth in the future.

  vi) A more accurate method of ascertaining size is the future value of profit. A business would wish to know that if it pays, e.g., £5 million for another company it would be able to pay off that investment from the profit which results from the new, larger business.

5) Number of employees

  i) This is relatively easy to measure. It allows comparisons to be made across industries with regards to company size and whether the business is labour-intensive.

  ii) A labour-intensive company tends to have a higher percentage of labour costs in comparison with total costs.

  iii) The recent increase in the number of part-time workers has made labour-intensity less easy to calculate as it is not easy to equate part-time workers with full-time workers.

6) Market capitalisation

  i) This is calculated as follows:-

   No. of shares x Share price

  ii) Such a measure is one of the most frequently used for companies whose share price is quoted regularly on the various stock exchanges around the world.

  iii) The rising and falling share prices alter the value of a business.

iv) When the share price continually falls the company might be worried about a takeover bid, as this method of valuation is used when one company is bought by another.

v) When there is a takeover bid, the of fer for the shares is likely to value the company above its present market capitalization, in an effort to persuade the company's shareholders to sell the shares.

Why Is The Size Of A Business Important?

Business growth results in the following benefits:-

1) Customers are attracted to and "trust" the well-known larger businesses, though they might be charging higher prices.

2) The larger companies tend to get relatively better treatment and service from suppliers.

3) The larger companies tend to get better payment terms from suppliers.

4) The larger companies are more able to develop local community relations and sponsor local events.

Are There Any Advantages To Being A Small Company?

1) The small business is more flexible and could react to external changes more quickly, just like a speed boat being able to turn a corner faster than an ocean cruiser.

2) The press does enjoy ridiculing and criticizing the larger companies, e.g., over excessive executive pays, exploiting of staf, etc., which might result in a loss in sales. The larger companies therefore have to employ public relations staff to deal with the press, adding to their costs. The small business tends not to have such problems.

3) The small business is able to get close to its customers.

Economies Of Scale

1) Business might try to grow because they want to achieve economies of scale.

2) Economies of scale are defined as the decrease in unit cost as output increases.

3) With a reduction in unit cost, the company could either:-

   i) Reduce the price it chages (retaining the same profit magin) and sell more products.

   Or

   ii) Keep the price at the same level and earn more profit per unit.

4) The following are the various economies of scale:-

   i) Technical Economies Of Scale - As the business spreads its fixed costs across more units of output, the unit cost decreases.

   ii) Purchasing Economies Of Scale - As the business purchases more items from its suppliers, it might be possible to negotiate a bulk purchase discount.

iii) Technological Economies Of Scale - A business which buys a new, better machine enjoys increased efficiency, e.g., increased production speed, higher quality products and less wastage.

iv) Marketing Economies Of Scale - A large, reputable company such as Nestle and Heinz finds it easier and less expensive to market, as well as introduce, its products. The same advertisement promoting a generic brand name could also be used to promote the company's new products, with the advertising expenditure being spread across more products, thus reducing the unit cost for advertising.

v) Financial Economies Of Scale -A large company listed in the stock market enjoys status and prestige in the world of finance. Banks might be more willing to make loans to them and at a lower rate of interest too. The cost of raising finance is thus less expensive.

vi) Managerial Economies Of Scale -   The larger company which employs specialists to run the individual functions such as marketing, finance, production, etc., enjoys greater control over each function, which is more likely to lead to lower costs.

vii) Risk-bearing Economies Of Scale -   A growing business could diversify into other areas of business and might reduce its business risks in doing so. (Do not put all your eggs in one basket.)

viii) Specialisation Economies Of Scale - Specialisation, or, division of labour results in greater expertise and efficiency.

External

The growth of a company benefits other companies which have dealings with it as well as others, e.g., the company's suppliers getting more business from it, the local news agents and lunchtime snack bars.

Effects On Different Functions Of An Increase In Size

1) Marketing - An increase in sales volume or expansion into a new market would require more marketing resources, e.g., more marketing staf, new outlets and new wholesalers.

2) Production - A change in the scale or type of production and new machinery might be required.

3) Finance - Business expansion requires money for the purchase of materials and new machinery.

4) Management And Personnel - Business growth means that more staf are needed, e.g., shop floor operatives and specialist managers with greater skill levels. It is more difficult to run and control a larger organization.

Diseconomies Of Scale

It is not necessarily true that when output increases unit costs would decrease, due to the following reasons:-

1) The growing business might have to pay overtime or extra money for the staff working overtime. This would add to the unit cost as the output increases.

2) As business increases, machines might be made to run for longer periods of time than normal. This might lead to an increase in maintenance costs per unit.

3) Extra materials urgently ordered from suppliers might cost the company mor as the suppliers might charge higher prices for the urgent deliveries.

4) Business expansion might mean that co-ordination among the staf f and customers would become very difficult. Systems would then need to be put into place to ensure that the level of co-ordination and communication is appropriate. These extra co-ordination and communication cost money This might outweigh the benefits of size.

5) As the business grows the employees might feel neglected and less motivated. The or ganisation might become more bureaucratic (more paperwork) and its control might become much harder.

Limitations To Growth

1) Lack Of Market Growth - A company might have to expand into a new market if its present market stops growing, e.g., BritishAmerican Tobacco (BAT) diversified into financial services in the late 1980s, buying such companies as Allied Dunbar and Eagle Star Insurance, as there was very little prospect of growth in the tobacco market.

2) Lack Of Productive Capacity -   The business might need to turn away new orders, subcontract or prioritise present customers when it reaches full capacity, thereby compromising profit, customers and growth in some way.

3) Lack Of Finance - Finance is needed for growth both in the short and long term. Careful financial planning and ability to obtain loans from financial institutions are important.

4) Lack Of Trained S taff - An effective sales-force is important for the generation of revenue in the business, e.g., in the more specialised industries. Appropriate selection and training of sales staf f are thus important.

5) Objectives - The owner of the business might not want the business to grow for fear of losing control and challenge from the job.

Government Restrictions

1) Government interference might prevent businesses from joining together For example, the Trade and Industry Secretary prevented Rupert Murdoch's BskyB from buying Manchester United as he felt that the new company would not be in the best interest of all of its stakeholders.

2) A new government law might force the business to change something and thus hinder growth. For example, the introduction of minimum wage benefits many workers but threatens to reduce the profits of the company

44. FIRMS AND THEIR OBJECTIVES

The Importance Of Aims And Objectives

1) The short-term objectives of a company arise out of its main "goal".

2) The main "goal" of a company is called a mission statement.

Aims And Mission Statements

1) The mission statement gives the purpose of the business and is made known to all employees and shareholders.

2) Most mission statements stipulate the values of the business and its purpose.

3) The mission statement provides the framework for the operation of the business.

4) It has to be communicated effectively to the employees and constantly monitored to ensure that the purpose of the business is achieved.

5) An example of a mission statement is as follows:-

Diageo's Mission Statement

"Diageo is in business to create value for our shareholders by delighting our consumers all around the world."

6) For mission statements to be meaningful and effective the employees have to understand their purpose and be involved in their formulation.

7) The mission statement should indicate how the purpose of the business is to be achieved, which is helpful in understanding the tiers or hierarchy of objectives.

8) Everything else should be geared towards achieving the main aim of the business.

9) Using objectives, i.e., management by objectives, is an organisational tool and a method of ensuring that all employees are clear as to what is expected of them.

10) Management by objectives involves having a series of well-defined objectives which are designed to ensure that each part of the business is operating in an appropriate manner so that the main objective of the business is achieved.

11) Most businesses would have one of the following as their main aim:-

   i) Profit (especially for a major public listed company)

   ii) Survival (especially for a newly formed sole proprietorship)

   iii) Growth (other businesses)

12) A series of other objectives would need to be set in order to achieve a major objective.

13) Objectives provide a sense of direction and unity of purpose for the business. They also provide a measurement of performance that in turn could be used as an aid to control within the business.

14) However, the objectives of the different departments within the business might conflict with each other.

15) For example, if a mission statement states the desire to increase profit, an objective might have been set to cut costs.   The marketing department might have an objective to develop new products, whilst the finance department aims to reduce all the departmental budgets.

Strategy

1) A strategy is the method in which objectives are achieved.

2) To attain the main objectives, a business could have a strategy to achieve any of the following:-

   i)   A competitive advantage by having low costs.

   ii) Differentiating the product.

   iii) Increasing productivity.

3) Such a strategy is much more aimed for the short term and is often departmental, representing a functional aspect of the business.

4) Michael Porter, a Harvard Business School professor and an expert on strategies for competitive advantage, recommends that companies adopt a strategy which includes the following:-

   i)   Selling to the most sophisticated and demanding buyers.

   ii) Seeking out buyers with the most difficult needs.

   iii) Establishing norms of exceeding the toughest regulatory hurdles or product standards.

   iv) Sourcing from the most advanced and international home-based suppliers.

   v)   Treating employees as permanent instead of using a demoralising hire-and-fire approach.

   vi) Establishing outstanding competitors as motivators.

How Is Strategy Decided On?

1) Igor Ansoff, a professor at Carnegie, suggested that a business, in carrying out strategic planning, should identify a competitive advantage.

2) According to him, strategic planning should also be concerned about whether to continue with an existing product or develop a new product.

3) His ideas could be presented via a matrix, which is as follows:-

   Ansoff's Matrix

   Markets (Existing & New): Market Penetration & Market Development

   Products (New): Product Development & Diversification

4   Market penetration stipulates that the company sells a greater quantity of an existing product to consumers in an existing market, e.g., Kellogg tried to sell more cornflakes to existing consumers by promoting the idea of eating Kellogg's Cornflakes at any time of the day not just at breakfast.

5)   Market development involves selling an existing product to new customers, e.g., Brylcreme, a hair gel traditionally sold to the older consumer, was repackaged and promoted to the younger consumers with great success.

6)   Product development requires the company to sell a new product to existin consumers, e.g., Walkers has launched a range of new flavours for its crisps, for instance, Cheese and Owen.

7)   Diversification requires the company to develop a new product to be sold to new consumers, e.g., Mars has launched a range of ice-creams.

8)   All these decisions with regard to strategy should not be made in isolation.

9)   A company has to find out where its competitive advantage might be.

10) To do this and thus plan the most appropriate strategy , the marketing department might carry out a SWOT analysis, i.e., research into the Strengths, Weaknesses, Opportunities and Threats in order to arrive at the best strategy.

11) The strengths and weaknesses focus on internal factors.

12) For example, Cadbury Schweppes' conclusions after a SWOT analysis might be as follows:-

Strengths:

Well-established brand names including its most famous Cadbury's Dairy Milk, major brands in several of the chocolate market segments and a sound financial base.

Weaknesses:

Might be considered an old brand.

Opportunities:

Many confectionery businesses could be acquired, new markets (especially in Eastern Europe) are available and other market niches which could be exploited following the huge success of the introduction of Favourites into the "assortments" market.

Threats:

Major competitors, e.g., Nestle, continue to expand and compete with Cadbury's brands, the legal and economic climate in which Cadbury' s functions, health reports which highlight the dangers of eating too much chocolate and an economic downturn which reduces the amount spent on sweets.

13) Cadbury Schweppes' strategy relies on a value-based management technique, i.e., having a systematic way of analyzing and understanding a business, the market in which it operates, and, its strengths and its weaknesses and those of its competitors.

14) They then try to develop better strategies which would produce changes in the competitive performance.

15) After the strategy is formulated, the final layer of objectives could be put in place, i.e., the tactics which could be used to ensure that the strategy is successful.

Tactics

1) Tactics involve the implementation of the strategic plan on a day-to-day basis.

2) Each part of the strategic plan should be broken down into departmental secondary objectives with targets which could be measured.

3) For example, Cadbury's strategy for its confectionery is based on strengthening of their key brands through marketing investment and innovation in new product development.

4) Thus, its tactical objectives or secondary objectives might be to:-

   i) Increase the market budget for any new lines.

   ii) Attempt the launch of at least two new brands over the following financial year.

5) After establishing the various levels of objectives a simple summary is formulated, which is as follows:-

   The Hierarchy Of Objectives

   Mission statement or aim (the primary objective)

   Objectives which are necessary to fulfill the mission statement

   Strategy, the implementation of the objectives

   Tactics, for which targets are set and monitored

Corporate Culture

1) How the hierarchy of objectives is implemented is often dependent on th philosophy or culture of the business.

2) The corporate culture (or ethos) might lead to the formulation of the business plan, which the business might use to map out its delivery of its mission statement.

3) A company's objective might be to ensure that every staf f member is obsessed with delighting the customers and creating value for its shareholders.

4) It might ensure that everyone in the company has absolute clarity on where the company is heading.

5) The company is organised in such a way as to ensure that every aspect of the business is geared towards creating value for its shareholders.

6) This involves establishing a common way of defining what value is and how to create it.

7) The whole ethos or way in which the company is managed is geared towards the achievement of the company objective or objectives.

8) A company's statement of its purpose should be a reflection of its personality.

9) Many principles in a company's mission statements might be just repetitions of previous statements and could be perceived as mere soundbites and no more.

Contingency Plans

1) There would be occasions when external factors beyond the control of the company, if not addressed, would either permanently or temporarily prevent it from achieving its aim.

2) It is important to include a contingency plan in a business plan to deal with such unforeseen situations.

3) Many companies had to implement contingency plans to tackle the millennium bug in 2000. For example, most of the world's airlines in 2000 decided not to fly between the hours of 10 p.m. on New Year's Eve and 6 a.m. on New Year's Day, just in case the millennium bug hit the air traffic control computers. Many companies made contingency plans for the payment of their staff's wages and salaries and many banks stocked more cash than normal in anticipation of more cash withdrawals from customers who feared that the cash dispensers might malfunction. Microsoft had sold a range of software "patches" which could be used to ensure that personal computers did not crash.

4) If mission statements are to be meaningful, an "inclusive" approach should be adopted by the company.

5) This would require the company to:-
   i) define purpose and values
   ii) review key relationships
   iii) define success
   iv) measure and communicate performance
   v) reward and reinforce

6) It is important that companies establish their main aims or objectives, which should be measurable and clearly imparted to all the employees within the company.

Constraints

1) There would be problems which prevent a company's objectives from being met.

2) These problems sometimes force the company to change the objective.

3) These problems, which constrain the business, divide themselves into internal and external.

4) A company could frequently do something to rid itself of the cause of the internal constraint, but it has to react to the external constraint.

Internal Constraints

Legal Structure

1) Sole traders are frequently unable to obtain the finance they need to expand the business due to the lack of collateral.

2) Customers might also trust a sole trader less than a major, famous public listed company.

3) However, the sole trader could provide a personal service to the customer

Time

1) Investors in a public listed company normally look for a quick profit, quickly selling off their shares at a profit and investing their money elsewhere.

2) This has led to pressure being put on public listed companies to produce short-term profits, sometimes at the expense of long-term growth.

Geographical Location

1) A company operating in several countries might have difficulty co-ordinating their operations, e.g., due to poor telecommunications or the lack of an efficient telecommunication system which might be costly.

2) Markets, religion and cultures might be different and this might mean that a separate set of objectives has to be pursued, e.g., short-term profits are very hard to achieve in Japan as it requires a much longer time to deal with Japanese companies than anywhere else in the world.

Conflict Of Interests

1) New ideas in an organisation are likely to meet with some opposition as they result in a conflict of interests, e.g., the production manager's suggestion of getting a new machine, which would reduce the cost of production by a significant sum of money, might be costly to implement, and, though it could produce cheaper products for the marketing department to sell resulting in better sales, to the pleasure of the marketing manager, it might also mean that initially the marketing budget would be reduced.

2) It is considered important to meet the following three objectives: task, group and individual needs.

3) For example, if a product manager 's ambition to be promoted is not recognised by his company, there could be the following repercussions:-

    i) The individual would not perform the task well, possibly resulting in a loss of market share.

    ii) His sales teams might pick up on the bad feeling and do not perform well.

Finance

1) There is normally a constraint on the availability of finance, resulting in the company not being able to carry out everything that it wishes to do and tighter financial control.

2 For example, a reduction in the advertising or marketing budget in preference of increasing the budget in another aspect of the business.

External Constraints

1) A business has very little control over the external environment, which would thus affect the achievement of its objectives.

2) It might have to alter its objectives if an external constraint is too significant to avoid. Competition

1) The strength of competition depends on the relative sizes of the competing companies, e.g., in 1999, BP joined with Amoco and Texaco joined with Chevron in order to compete more effectively against each other.

2 Companies frequently try to outdo each other in terms of size in order to wipe out any competitive advantage resulting from an increase in size.

3) The larger and therefore more influential company in the market-place would normally be the price leader , i.e., it sets a price which becomes standard fo the industry.

Government Policy (Local And National)

1) The primary aim of the town and borough councils (at the local level) is to provide services to the community.

2) A business intending to extend its premises in order to expand needs planning approval from these authorities which could take many weeks to obtain and which might even be refused ultimately.

3) The national government sets laws which could impinge on a business, such as increasing value added tax (VAT), which would push up the prices of products, making them less attractive to customers and thus affecting its sales revenue, and, passing environmental laws which require the business to invest in pollution control equipment, which would add to its costs without being likely to add value.

Economic

1) As the economy moves into recession, any plans for a business expansion might have to be delayed.

2) Rising interest rates could make an investment too expensive relative to the expected return.

Ethics

1) In recent years, companies have had to be more conscious of ethical issues in the way they operate.

2) The concern about human rights in some countries, the exploitation of cheap labour and environmental problems has af fected the conduct of business, e.g., where a business locates overseas.

45. STAKEHOLDERS IN THE ECONOMY

The Stakeholder Economy

1) A stakeholder in a country is any person, business or public sector organisation, which is affected by a decision of a government, directly or indirectly.

2) The stakeholders in a country comprise of the following:-
   i) International community
   ii) Ethnic minorities
   iii) Business and employees
   iv) Unemployed
   v) Old-age pensioners
   vi) The sick
   vii) Teachers and students
   viii) Armed forces

3) Similarly, businesses have to become more aware of the various stakeholders.

4) A stakeholder in an organisation is a person or organisation which has an interest in the actions and reactions of a particular business.

5) The actions of a business would have a direct or indirect efect on others.

6) A business might have any of the following stakeholders:-
   i) Government
   ii) Banks
   iii) Managers and directors
   iv) Retailers and wholesalers
   v) Unions

vi)   Customers

vii)   Shareholders

viii) Employees and dependents

ix)   Suppliers and subcontractors

x)   Competition

xi)   Community

xii)   Consumer organisations

Stakeholders (In Alphabetical Order)

Banks

1)   How successful a business is could af fect the success of the bank from which it has obtained some loan.

2)   Should the business fail, the bank might take over the ownership of some of the business's assets and sell them off.

3)   The bank would normally bring in the receivers to wind up the business if it is not confident that the business would repay the principal sum originally lent.

Community

1)   The community comprises not only the local community but also environmental groups who campaign for the protection of the environment, locally or globally.

2)   Retrenchment by a lar ge company could result in many people in the community being unemployed, leading to social problems.

3)   The supporting and other industries, e.g., the lar ge company's suppliers and other providers of services, ranging from small grocers to garages and car mechanics, would also be affected by the retrenchment.

4)   The environmental pressure groups also keep an eye on businesses to see that their business activities do not cause environmental problems.

Competition

1)   A business launching a successful product would not only reduce the competitors' market share, but might also prompt competitors to copy their products and emulate their marketing strategies, e.g., the competition between Tesco and Sainsbury.

2)   A new initiative by a company, e.g., extra free bars or lar ger bars of the same price, is quickly followed by competitors.

Customers

1)   Customers would like a business to succeed as it would mean a continual flow of new, advanced, competitive products, greater choice and lower prices.

2) Many companies spend considerable time retaining customer loyalty through careful marketing and research. Customer loyalty depends on the product being sold and on the individual.

3) Customers expect consistent quality and prices.

4) Customers expect the same price for the same product. It would be irritating for them to find the same product they bought for £,000, e.g., reduced in price to £800 two weeks later.

Consumer Organisations

1) Consumer organisations, e.g., The Consumers' Association, normally attempt to guide the consumer to the best product in terms of value for money and also seek to represent customers who have been badly treated by companies, as well as provide advice which is free and independent.

Employees And Dependents

1) If the company is profitable, their employees are likely to enjoy more pay and/or greater security and possibly profit-sharing schemes. The employees' families would also indirectly benefit. This is often the case with Japanese companies which are paternalistic toward their employees.

2) Less scrupulous companies might insist on longer hours and shorter contracts and might not reward loyalty and skill with the appropriate levels of pay.

Government

1) A business has to pay several different types of tax to the government, e.g., income tax, corporate tax and national insurance would represent most of the tax.

2) Other taxes include value added tax, which would be paid by most companies, fuel duty, which would be paid by a petrol retailer, tax or excise duty on alcohol, which would be paid by a publican, tax on dividends and customers duties on imported goods.

3) Should a business fail, the government would lose tax revenue and would also have to increase its expenditure on unemployment benefit.

Managers And Directors

1) Some company managers and directors might also be shareholders besides being stakeholders, i.e., they might have been awarded share options or might just own shares in the company.

2) The future prospects of most managerial staff would depend on the success of the company, e.g., its market share, profit and share price.

3) Some staff would be evaluated by sales results while other staff, e.g., production managers, by productivity levels.

4) The more senior the position of the director is, the more rewards (in terms of bonuses) he would receive, though the riskier his job would become,

as he might be removed from office if the shareholders failed to be impressed by his performance.

Retailers/Wholesalers

1) A retailer or wholesaler (middleman) might stock a particular product or might be the sole distributor of a particular brand.

2) A successful manufacturer might depend much on a retailer and allow it to stock more products, perhaps at a lower cost.

3) Manufacturers might also spend much money promoting and advertising their products, thus benefiting the wholesalers and retailers.

4) The successful promotion and advertising by the manufacturers also bring in greater sales revenue to the wholesalers and retailers.

Shareholders

1) Shareholders, as the owners of the business, would be aiming to achieve two important financial goals, viz., some form of capital gain (where the share price increases above its purchase price) and dividends.

2) Shareholders take the risk as investors in the business, i.e., if the business fails they would be last to get their money back.

3) As a result, the shareholders normally study the financial performance of the company carefully.

4) There are shareholders who adopt an "ethical" stand when making their investment, e.g., investing only in environmentally friendly companies.

Suppliers And Subcontractors

1) Nowadays, out-sourcing or subcontracting part of the company's activities to other companies, while carrying out the core or main part of the business in-house, is common.

2) Subcontractors would grow in number and could become more efficient in their respective specialist functions.

3) The company's suppliers would of course benefit if the company does well.

4) The company's suppliers would be concerned about being punctually paid and their cash flow depends much on their major customers.

Unions

1) Unions could take action regardless of the success of the business.

2) How active the unions are would depend on whether the employees are satisfied at the work-place.

3) When the company does well and takes good care of its employees the unions are less likely to cause problems.

4) The unions, however, tend to be unpredictable and might then bargain for even greater wage increases.

Potential For Conflicts

1) A business has to realise that it is almost impossible to satisfy all stakeholders all the time.

2) It might be possible to satisfy all of the stakeholders some of the time or some of the stakeholders all the time.

3) The following are a few examples:-

Example 1

Due to a cash flow problem, the company gives an extended credit period to a large customer, while not paying a supplier on timeThe company gives priority to the large customer at the expense of the supplier.

Example 2

Company directors receive large profit-related bonuses for having saved money for the company by sacking ten per cent of the work-force. There is conflict between employees, unions and directors. Some customers who feel strongly about this might not continue to purchase from the company.

Example 3

A business donates money to the local community at the expense of the dividend paid to the shareholders. The affected shareholders might resent it.

Example 4

A business sponsors a charity by contributing a certain percentage of its revenue. This could be construed as helping the communityBut the more cynical business observers might think that the business is doing so for its own promotional ends.

Critics And Supporters

Those In Favour

John Neill, the managing director at Unipart, is a great supporter of the stakeholders theory. He believes in a close working relationship between the company, its employees and its suppliers. He encourages long-term commitment from all the company' s stakeholders so that there would be a continual commitment to reduce waste and, thus, costs, and improve quality and profitability.

Those Against

The flamboyant chairman of the Dixons Group which owns a chain of high street and retail warehousing shops selling electrical goods, Sir Sanley Kalms, has always seen the business world as cut-throat and merciless. He thinks showing mercy is likely to be seen as a sign of weakness and, as the markets his business operates in are highly competitive, he has to be equally without mercy He keeps his suppliers at arm' s length, giving them no security of contract beyond the short term. He believes that the insecurity would make the suppliers fight harder. He also pays his employees a minimum basic salary and expects them to fight hard for customer sales, on which they earn commission.

Stakeholder Evaluation

1) The objectives of a company would vary according to the demands or requirements of its stakeholders.

2) A business decision might affect some stakeholder more than the others, and therefore, the business has to prioritise the stakeholder , given the particular situation.

3) This means that the business has to decide which is the most important objective to achieve.

4) For example, ice-cream is not considered a healthy food, but a new company might sell ice-cream from vans which visit schools in order to achieve sales. In this case, the company's priority is sales revenue, which is needed for the company to survive.

46. BUSINESS FINANCE

Financial Sources

1) Funds for the financing of business activities are obtainable from banks, e.g., DBS Bank, OCBC Bank and UOB, or from finance companies, e.g., Hong Leong Finance and Singapura Finance.

2) They are also obtained by selling ordinary shares to private individuals on a personal basis, or , selling bonds or ordinary shares to the public through the stock exchange, e.g., the Stock Exchange of Singapore.

3) They could also be obtained from the parent companies overseas.

4) Funds are classified into short term and long term funds, and, debt funds and equity funds.

Short Term Finance

1) Short term financing consists of the funds a company has to repay within a year of obtaining those funds, e.g., trade credits given by suppliers, deposits and advances from customers, short term loans from banks, finance companies, factoring companies or insurance companies, etc..

Spontaneous Short Term Financing

1) The company can rely on credit extended by the supplier for goods purchased.

2) The consequence for delaying payment to suppliers are that the supplier may be reluctant to supply the company goods in future, or , if they do, may charge higher prices for the goods supplied.

3) Trade credits as a source of finance can be very expensive if discounts are not taken into account.

4) Another spontaneous short term financing is available when the company delays payments for some of its expenses, e.g., wages and salaries, rents, taxes and utilities (water and electrical bills).

Unsecured Short Term Financing

1) The company may be able to obtain unsecured short term loans from banks (which do not require collateral), e.g., overdraft or line of credit, revolving credit agreement, letter of credit and transaction loan, which are as follows:-

   a) Line Of Credit Or Overdraft

   The line of credit or overdraft is an arrangement made between the company and the bank whereby the bank agrees to give a certain amount of credit to the company The interest on this type of loan is based on the amount of overdraft used by the company , and, this interest is worked out on a daily basis. This is the cheapest form of financing for a company but the company must maintain its credit worthiness.

   b) Revolving Credit Agreement

   The revolving credit agreement is similar to the overdraft but the bank makes a formal and legally binding commitment to extend credit to the company up to the agreed amount of credit.   The company is required to pay a commitment fee to the bank for the privilege of having funds made available to it on demand.

   c) Letter Of Credit

   The letter of credit is a written undertaking to the exporter through the corresponding bank pledging that payment will be made for goods supplied, provided that the exporter complies with the terms of the letter of credit. Once payment has been made by the issuing bank, the sum becomes a loan from the bank to the importer , and this is usually a revolving credit arrangement.   The importer may have to make a small or lar ge deposit (depending on its credit worthiness) at the bank.

   d) Transaction Loan

   A transaction loan is a loan given by a bank to a company to finance the latter's transaction when the latter has a firm order on handThe loan must be repaid as soon as payment is received from the contract. Such loans are very common for small companies in Singapore, especially contractors. The interest rates on unsecured loans vary from company to company and from bank to bank, depending on the borrowing company's credit worthiness.

Secured Short Term Financing

1) If the company could furnish suf ficient security for the amount of loan

required, it would not be hard to obtain credit facilities from a bank or a finance company.

2) The following secured short term financing may be obtainable:-

a) Accounts Receivable Financing

Collateral, e.g., trade debts, inventories or stocks, share certificates, marketable securities, fixed deposit certificates, machinery and equipment, or, personal guarantees of shareholders, is required.The bank or finance company interested in giving the loan to the company would evaluate the quality of the receivables of fered as collateral and then establish a loan value for the receivables. The borrowing company is required to give an undertaking to the bank or finance company to remit all payments for these receivables, to of fset the loan balance.

b) Factoring Of Accounts Receivable

Also, items under the collateral (receivables) could be sold to a bank, a finance company, or, a factoring company to raise short term funds. The company sells its receivables to a factor (a bank, finance company or factoring company), which would then be responsible for collecting the accounts receivable and bearing the risk of bad debts. Factoring enables a company to grant credit to its customers without much risk, as the factor would check on the credit worthiness of the customers before it decides to buy the company' s accounts receivable.

c) Inventory Financing

Short term loans could also be obtained by pledging inventories. The loan value for inventories depends on the perishability , marketability and price stability of the inventories pledged, which could take the following forms:

i) Trust Receipt Loan (Bridging Loan or MerchandiseAdvance)

This is a loan given by a bank against specific inventories which remain in the possession of the companyThe borrowing company is required to sign a trust receipt indicating that it is holding the goods on trust for the bank and, at the same time, is required to accept a time bill drawn on it for a fixed period for the full cost of the goods.

ii) Terminal Warehouse Receipt Loan

The lending bank requires that the inventories of the borrowing company be stored in a bonded public warehouse before it grants the loan. The borrowing company cannot sell any of the goods stored in the public warehouse without the bank' s written permission.

iii)   Field Warehouse Receipt Loan

The field warehouse receipt loan is similar to the terminal warehouse receipt loan arrangement, except that the goods, which are too bulky to be conveniently stored in a bonded warehouse, are stored in the borrowing company' s premises instead of a bonded warehouse.

iv)   Floating Lien Loan

The borrowing company pledges all its inventories without any specific identification of the inventory item involved as collateral for the loan. A floating charge is very general and a bank finds it difficult to monitor this type of loan and would normally not lend heavily against it. There is the problem of the liquidation of the collateral.

v)   Endorsed Loans or Bank Guarantees

A company may be able to obtain a short term loan if the principal shareholders or some other parties acceptable to the bank stand as guarantors for the loan (they give a written undertaking to the bank that they would make good the loan if the borrowing company defaults).   The guarantees could be specific or continuing.

d)   Monetary Authority of Singapore Rediscounting Scheme

A company in the exporting business can obtain funds by discounting its pre-export and export usuance bills of exchange under the MAS Rediscounting Scheme (the MAS interest rate is lower than the prevailing lending rate of banks). The exporting company does not obtain the finance direct from MAS but through its bank, which acts as intermediary between the company and the MAS (the bank receives a commission for the discounting of the bill)The company obtains the following proceeds by discounting its bills:

Proceeds = [Face Value - (Face Value x Rate Of Interest x No. Of Days)] ÷ 365

Long Term Finance

Hire-purchase Finance

A company buying a fixed asset on hire-purchase could enter into an agreement with either the vendor of the asset or a finance company and agree to make a down payment and regular periodic installment payments for the use of the vendor's or the finance company's asset. There is no need to pledge any form of security and the company is able to enjoy depreciation allowances on the equipment, even though technically it does not own the asset. Hire-purchase is expensive and the asset would be repossessed if the company could not keep up with the installments.

Lease Financing

Lease financing could be obtained for the renting of equipment.An agreement is entered into between the company and the owner of the equipment, which may state that the company can neither return the asset nor refuse to pay the rental payments within the lease period (financial lease), or , it may state that the company has the option to return the equipment upon giving due notice to the owner (operating lease).The company is able to obtain the use of a piece of equipment without having to buy it.The company could also obtain finance by selling the expensive equipment it owns to another party and then leasing it back from this party (sale and lease-back).

Fixed Or Term Loans

Fixed or term loans are loans with a maturity period of more than a year obtained by pledging some of the company's assets, e.g., land and properties, fixed deposit certificates, foreign currencies, and, stocks and shares of public listed companies, as collateral for the loan (term loan or fixed loan).The borrowing company has to make regular monthly, quarterly or yearly installment payments to retire the loan and to pay for the interest chages. The borrowing company could arrange with the lender to work out a payment schedule that is geared to its cash flow ability to service the debt. The interest rate on a fixed or term loan is generally higher than the rate chaged for overdraft facilities. Because of the higher risks, a bank or finance company may require a borrowing company to comply with a number of conditions, which are as follows:-

a) Maintain proper accounting records and regularly submit audited financial statements to the lender.

b) Maintain a certain amount of working capital during the loan period.

c) Limit capital expenditure on new equipment and machinery to a certain level.

d) Stop incurring any additional long term debt.

e) Limit its cash dividends payment to a certain percentage of earnings.

f) Use the loan only for the purpose it was granted.

The loan agreement entered into between the borrowing company and the lending company may also restrict the borrowing company from factoring its accounts receivable or entering into long term financial leases.

Bond And Debenture Issues

Certificates of indebtedness are given to members of the public as evidence of the issuing company's debt to the holders of these certificates. Bonds are loans secured by a lien on some specific assets of the company while debentures are unsecured or general credit bonds.The following are the main features of bonds and debentures:-

a) They are usually issued in $1,000 units, though smaller or lar ger denominations are possible, which is known as the par value of the bonds or debentures.

b) They usually carry a fixed interest rate, known as the coupon rate, which may be paid to the holders either half-yearly or annually.

c) They have a fixed maturity date, which is some time in the future, when the principal sum specified on the certificates would be paid back to the holders.

d) The maturity date, or, repayment date varies among issues.

To make these bonds attractive, the company may sometimes make them convertible (option to be converted into ordinary shares of the company at some future date, at a stated conversion rate. Many types of bonds could be issued (but very few are issued in Singapore).

Preference Shares

Preference shares are a hybrid between bonds and ordinary shares, and, are shares that carry certain preferences over ordinary shares. The following are the main features of preference shares:-

a) They represent ownership in the company and are part of the company's net worth.

b) There is no fixed maturity date, unlike bonds.

c) They do not carry voting rights, which may however be gained by the preference shares holders if the company fails to pay them their dividends.

d) If the preference shares are convertible, they may be converted into ordinary shares.

e) Dividends paid on preference shares are usually fixed and cumulative. But, in some cases, the dividends paid on the preference shares may be "participating", i.e., the holders of these shares, besides receiving the regular dividends, also participate with the holders of ordinary shares in any remaining dividends.

f) Should the company be liquidated, the preference shareholders have prior claims on the company's assets over the ordinary shareholders.

The following are some advantages which accrue to a company that obtains capital by issuing preference shares:-

a) There is leverage, i.e., obtaining funds at a fixed cost (because of the fixed dividend rate) and possibly using them elsewhere in the business to get high rates of return.

b) Funds are obtainable at no fixed charge as dividends are paid at the discretion of the board of directors.

c) Funds are obtainable at a cost that is below equity cost as the risk of buying bonds is lower than that of buying ordinary shares.

d)   There is management control as funds are obtainable without having to grant voting rights to the subscribers of these shares.

e)   The company's equity base is widened as preference shares are considered part of its net worth, which permits greater borrowing.

The following are the two main disadvantages of issuing preference shares:-

a)   This type of funds is obtained at a higher cost than that of bonds.

b)   Dividends paid are not tax deductible, which thus raises the cost of this type of financing.

Ordinary Shares

Ordinary shares represent ownership interests in the company . Ordinary shareholders, as owners of the company, have complete and final claim to the remaining profits of the company after all the other classes of debt and equity claimants have received their specified returns. Ordinary shares may or may not have a stated par value, which is arbitrary Like preference shares, ordinary shares have no maturity date. Except in the case of bankruptcy or a reorganisation, the ordinary shareholders cannot be forced to give up their rights. The ordinary shareholders have voting rights; they may vote for members of the board of directors of the company. They also have pre-emptive rights, i.e., rights to purchase new ordinary shares in the same proportion as their current ownership interest.

47.   PUBLIC FINANCE

1)   Public expenditure is the amount spent by the central government, local authorities and public corporations, e.g. on goods, services, grants, subsidies and interest payments on national savings and government bonds (repayment of the national debt).

2)   An increase in public expenditure could af fect the rate of inflation (resulting in demand pull inflation) while a decrease in public expenditure could have deflationary effects.

3)   An increase in public expenditure could reduce unemployment and probably cause a shortage of labour while a decrease in public expenditure could cause unemployment.

4)   The pattern of expenditure is important, e.g., capital spent on motorways increases employment, capital expended on the purchase of buildings housing government offices previously rented has no efect on employment levels and certain industries could be encouraged or discouraged by government contracts and subsidies, e.g., building and construction.

4)   An increase in government spending might involve an increase in the public sector borrowing requirement (PSBR) which has important

inflationary effects, and, such a high level of spending must relate to a high level of income.

5) The government could adopt the following three options:-

   i) Have a balanced budget whereby government expenditure equals government income.

   ii) Have a deficit budget whereby government expenditure exceeds government income, making borrowing necessary (could be deliberate policy for raising employment levels).

   iii) Have a surplus budget whereby government income exceeds government spending (could be deliberate policy to take money out of the economy in order to reduce the rate of inflation).

Sources Of Government Income

The government obtains income from direct and indirect taxes, which are the most important source of government revenue.

Direct Taxes

The following are the various forms of direct taxes:-

1) Proportional (percentage of income taxed remains constant regardless of income level) and progressive (percentage of income taxed increases with the increase in income level) tax, levied on individuals and partnerships.

2) Corporation tax, levied on a company's profits.

3) Capital gains tax, levied on the disposal/sale of capital, e.g., shares, paintings, etc..

4) Capital transfer tax, levied on gifts made during the life or on the estate of a deceased person (replaces estate duty/death duties).

5) The following are the advantages of direct taxation:-

   i) Socially just - those earning lower incomes pay no tax or a smaller proportion of their incomes in tax than those earning higher incomes.

   ii) Provides a means of income redistribution - money in the form of taxes collected from the higher income groups could be distributed to the poorer sections of the community in the form of various benefits, e.g., family income supplements, child allowances, etc..

   iii) Could assist the government's economic policy - a reduction in taxes could generate increased expenditure in times of unemployment while an increase in taxes could reduce aggregate demand in times of inflation.

   iv) The tax does not directly cause inflation.

   v) The tax is easy and relatively cheap to collect and it is easy to predict the amount which would be collected.

6) The disadvantages of direct taxation are as follows:-

    i)   It is a great disincentive to effort. (People might not want to work hard if increased wages and profits are heavily taxed.)

    ii)   Efficient firms lose out when efficiency results in higher profits that are subject to a high level of taxation.

    iii)   As a result, investment might be adversely affected and might be diverted overseas.

    iv)   High taxation might reduce the level of foreign investments.

    v)   The higher income groups save a higher proportion of their incomes than the lower income groups, and, if the higher income groups are heavily taxed the level of savings would fall, which would have wide-ranging economic effects, e.g., on investment.

    vi)   High levels of direct taxation could result in tax avoidance.

Indirect Taxes

All indirect taxes are regressive, i.e., the lower income groups pay a higher proportion of their incomes in indirect taxes (a higher percentage of their incomes is paid in indirect taxes than do the higher income groups). The following are the various kinds of indirect taxes:-

1)   Value added tax (VAT), levied on all goods and services at all stages of their production process, possibly with a few exceptions.

2)   Excise duty, levied on petrol, alcohol, tobacco and other home produced goods.

3)   Customs duty, levied on goods imported into the country.

4)   Betting duties, levied on forms of gambling, e.g., horse racing and football pools.

5)   Rates, levied by the local authorities on properties within the local authorities' areas.

6)   The following are the advantages of indirect taxation:-

    i)   Income earners retain a higher proportion of their incomes at source. (This provides an incentive to hard work and effort, which should be economically beneficial to society.)

    ii)   This gives rise to the element of personal choice as consumers could decide whether to pay the indirect taxes or not by choosing to buy or not to buy the goods in question.

    iii)   The government could selectively manipulate the economy , e.g., encouraging or discouraging certain industries, or , reducing the demand for imported goods, by adjusting the levels of indirect taxation.

    iv)   It is an economic weapon which could bring immediate results, e.g., a reduction in the demand for oil could be achieved quickly by an increase in the tax on petrol.

7) The disadvantages of indirect taxation are as follows:-

   i) Indirect taxes are regressive (as described above).

   ii) An increase in indirect taxes has immediate inflationary effects as the prices of goods and services immediately go up (together with the increase in indirect taxes).

   iii) Indirect taxation could dislocate the market equilibrium by distorting the supply conditions.

   iv) Indirect taxation results in much administrative and clerical work on the part of both the businesses and the civil service, e.g., VAT has been found to be expensive to collect and has proven to be greatly onerous to the small firms.

   v) Firms that are in the early stages of development are not able to obtain tax relief and this might hamper their growth.

Other Sources Of Government Income

Besides taxes, the following are the other sources of government income:-

   i) Trading surpluses - include profits from public corporations, income of water authorities and similar organisations and rent from corporation houses.

   ii) National insurance contributions - income from the compulsory national insurance contributions from all workers in full-time or part-time employment or self-employment.

   iii) Motor vehicle and other licences - include "road tax", fees for passports and licences for dogs and guns.

   iv) Borrowings - short term government borrowings such as treasury bills and long term government borrowings such as government stock (gilts). (The amount the government needs to borrow annually is known as the public sector borrowing requirement (PSBR). Accumulated government borrowings over the years constitute the national debt.)

Steps Against Poverty

1) Much government expenditure is spent on reducing the efects of income inequality by giving help to those people who need it, e.g., through clothing allowances, rent allowances, rate rebates, free school meals, free prescriptions, family income supplements, etc..

2) Many of these benefits are income-related, i.e., only those whose incomes are below a certain level qualify for the benefits.

3) There could be a situation whereby an increase in earnings, which disqualifies a person from enjoying such benefits, is not as beneficial as

the benefits themselves, and, it would be better for the person to enjoy the benefits rather than the increase in earnings, i.e., the benefits would be a disincentive to some people to work hard and increase their earnings.

4) This situation could happen because the diferent government departments use different income scales for granting benefits and because the scales are not changed frequently enough to keep pace with inflation.

48. ECONOMIC DEVELOPMENT

1) Objective of study of economics: Achieve greater economic growth, development and welfare in an economy.

2) Definitions and concept:-

a) Economic growth: Real changes in production of goods and services, measured as gross domestic product (GDP) or gross national product (GNP), i.e., quantitative growth

b) Economic development: Concerns both quantitative growth (a necessary condition) and qualitative improvements such as the physical quality of life, which could be made possible with a certain amount of fair income distribution.

c) Economic welfare: Result of economic development. Things which contribute to economic welfare include items such as home production and anti-pollution measures. (Things which detract from welfare, such as pollution, are presently not accounted for in the GDP.)

d) Physical quality of life: Literacy , life expectancy, infant mortality rate, etc..

e) Standard of living: Measured by per capita GDP or per capita GNP.

3) The study of economics helps people to achieve a higher standard of living.

4) When comparing standards of living between countries the following are looked at:-

Economic Indicators

a) Real growth of GDP or GNP.

b) GDP or GNP per capita.

c) Demography and population.

d) Income distribution and equity.

e) Labour and employment.

f) Human development index - a composite weighted index of real GDP literacy and infant mortality rate.

g) Inflation.

Physical Indicators

a)   Food intake in calories.

b)   Water and sanitation.

c)   Living space.

Social Indicators

a)   Education and human resource development.

b)   Health.

c)   Transport and communication, i.e., accessibility to goods and services.

d)   Housing and living conditions.

e)   Environment and pollution.

Political Indicators

a)   Political freedom.

b)   Human rights.

c)   Civil liberty.

5)   In the developing economies these indicators are likely to have relatively low or unfavourable values.

6)   The developing economies are likely to have the following characteristics:-

a)   Dominance by the primary sector in the industrial structure.

b)   High population growth and dependency ratio.

c)   Large rural population and high levels of unemployment and underemployment.

d)   Employment in primary sector only declines as secondary and tertiary sectors begin to emerge.

e)   Inequitable income distribution as measured by the Lorenz curve Gini coefficient.

f)   High dependence on external trade.

g)   High dependence on foreign capital and technology.

h)   Dominance by subsistence agriculture rather than commercial activities.

i)   Traditional cultures and values hinder the application of science and technology in agriculture.

j)   Land fragmentation and "absentee" landlords are some of the factors causing low productivity.

7)   The following are the benefits of industrialisation:-

a)   Creation of employment and income.

b)   It uses up the surplus labour from agriculture.

95

c) It is the engine of growth.

d) It is export oriented and earns foreign exchange.

e) Industrial goods are more price elastic both in terms of demand and supply and have higher income elasticities, and, all this favours them as commodities for export.

f) It is more amenable to the application of science and technology , technology transfer, skills training and on-the-job-training.

g) Production for local consumption reduces imports in the initial stage, and this saves foreign exchange.

8) The following are the benefits derived from agriculture:-

a) When the agricultural surplus is exported the country gains in foreign exchange.

b) Surpluses in food, raw materials and labour.

c) More income is earned resulting in availability of finance.

d) Has demand for goods from the industrial sector.

9) The causes of the problem of a developing economys' low level of economic growth is the low productivity of the agricultural sector.

10) The factors responsibility for the low productivity in the agricultural sector are as follows:-

a) Unwillingness to experiment or adopt new technologies due to traditional habits and culture.

b) Lack of supporting industries, e.g., credit and agricultural extension services.

c) Inefficient marketing and distribution systems.

d) Low investment and poor application of science and technology.

e) Poor incentives because of lack of land reform and "absentee" landlords.

f) Land fragmentation because of culture and traditional practice of subdividing land (inheritance).

11) Generally, low economic growth and development are caused by the following:-

a) Inadequate infrastructure.

b) Poor organisation and management, e.g., bureaucracy is inefficient and corrupt.

c) Large population and demographic structure, which result in high dependency.

d) Low incomes which result in low saving rates and a low level of finance.

12) According to the vicious cycle theory economic growth could be impeded when there is a supply bottleneck or a demand obstacle.

13) The following could be carried out to induce growth:-

   a) Economic planning.

   b) Foreign aid and overseas development assistance policies.

   c) Policies for enhancing and mobilising domestic saving and taxation.

   d) Mobilisation or augmenting of financial resources for growth.

   e) Developing the infrastructure.

   f) The strong role of government.

   g) Policies pertaining to population and demography.

49. INFLATION AND UNEMPLOYMENT

1) Under the Phillips curve, inflation and unemployment were found to be related.

2) The various phases of a business cycle correlate to shifts in aggregate demand, giving rise to a relationship between GNP and unemployment (Okun's Law) and unemployment and inflation (Phillips curve).

3) The following are theories of the business cycle:-

   i)   The accelerator theory

   ii)   The political cycle

   iii) The sunspot theory

4) The following shows the relationship between the general price level and the rate of inflation:-

$$\text{Rate of inflation} = \frac{\text{Price level (t) - Price level (t - 1)}}{\text{Price level (t - 1)}} \times 100\%$$

where t and t - 1 represent two time periods.

5) The following are the different degrees of inflation:-

   i)   Moderate inflation

   ii)   Hyperinflation

   iii) Galloping inflation

6) The following are the effects and costs of inflation:-

   i)   Distortions in income and wealth distribution

   ii)   Adverse macroeconomic effects in business cycle on output and employment

   iii) Adverse microeconomic effects on economic efficiency

   iv)   Distortion of resource allocation

   v)   Distortion or destruction of work effort and incentives

97

vi) Distortions of relative prices

vii) Distortions of long term arrangements and contracts such as collective agreements

viii) Socio-political costs

7) The following are the types and causes of inflation:-

   i) Demand-pull inflation

   ii) Cost-push inflation

   iii) Imported inflation

   iv) Inertial rate of inflation

8) The following are controls on inflation:-

   i) Fiscal policies

   ii) Monetary policies

   iii) Cost of living adjustment (COLA)

   iv) Price boards

9) The following are the types of price indices used for measuring inflation:-

   i) Consumer price index (CPI)

   ii) GNP or GDP deflator

   iii) Indices of retail prices of selected goods

   iv) Domestic supply price index

   v) Indices of imports and exports

   vi) Indices of locally manufactured goods

   vii) Indices of local and farm products

   viii) Indices of real estate property

   ix) Indices of building materials

10) The following are the types of unemployment:-

   i) Structural unemployment

   ii) Seasonal unemployment

   iii) Frictional unemployment

   iv) Cyclical unemployment

   v) Classical unemployment

   vi) Disguised unemployment

   vii) Regional unemployment

   viii) Natural unemployment (Depicted in the long run Phillips curve)

   ix) Voluntary and involuntary unemployment

   x) Underemployment

50. INTERNATIONAL TRADE

1) Theory of absolute advantage - two countries trade when one of them uses less resources than the other to produce a commodity.

2) Theory of comparative advantage - trade between two countries is based on a difference in their relative opportunity costs of producing a commodity.

3) Hecksher-Ohlin theorem - trade between two countries is based on comparative advantage (comparative advantage = lower factor cost in one country resulting from its being endowed with more of this factor than the other country).

4) Theorem of factor price equalisation - trade between two countries arises as the increase in demand for a certain factor owing to trade, increases its price; it is the difference in factor prices, i.e., costs in production of the commodity, which gives the country with the lower factor cost comparative advantage over the other.

5) Terms of trade = Ratio of the price of exports to the price of imports

6) The following are characteristics of the terms of trade:-

   i) Determined by relative bargaining strength of the trading partners.

   ii) A country would always prefer the other country's pre-trade terms of trade that are the cheapest.

   iii) Terms of trade for raw materials or primary goods are lower or less favourable compared to those for manufactured items. iv) Small, open trading economies are often price-takers and are unable to influence world prices.

7) The following are classifications for gains from trade:-

   i) Static gains - gains from exchange (larger production and consumption), gains from trade (division of labour), gains from specialisation, vent-for-surplus production

   ii) Dynamic gains - capital or investment inflow, technology transfer, movement of people and exchange in cultures and values

   iii) Trade as an engine of growth

8) Free trade is best option in economic terms.

9) Non-economic and political factors lead to protectionism.

10) Protectionism may be desirable for the infant industry when other forms of assistance cannot be employed.

11) Protectionism should be stopped once the infant industry can stand on its own; otherwise there will not be any incentive for it to be cost effective or quality conscious.

12) Protectionism leads to retaliation by others.

13) The other undesirable economic activities or actions include the following:-

    i)   Non-tariff barriers, e.g., dumping

    ii) Self-sufficiency, i.e., autarchy

    iii) Political embargo

    iv) Strategic trade policy or industrial policy

    v)   Mercantilist trade favouring exports

    vi) "Sweatshop" labour

14) There are two kinds of trade barriers (protectionism) - tariff barriers, and, non-tariff barriers (NTBs).

15) The impact of a tarif f can be analysed with a diagram in the following areas:-

    i)   Government revenue

    ii) Welfare loss as in consumer surplus, consumption loss and production loss or inefficiency

16) The following are non-tarif f barriers (also known as areas of grey protection):-

    i)   Quotas

    ii) International cartels

    iii) Export subsidies

    iv) Dumping

    v)   Voluntary export restraints or orderly marketing arrangements

    vi) Technical, administrative and other regulations

17) The following four stages represent how economic integration between countries could be carried out:-

    i)   Establishment of a customs union (a free trade area where all member countries impose a common external tarif f on non-member countries).

    ii) Establishment of an economic community (a common market with harmonised monetary and fiscal policies).

    iii) Establishment of a preferential trading agreement (selective preferential tariff reductions).

    iv) Establishment of a fine trade area (area where there is complete tariff liberalisation between member countries but each member country imposes its respective tariffs on non-member countries).

18) The objectives of economic integration are trade creation and trade diversion.

19) For a successful customs union to be possible the following conditions are to be present:-

   i)   Large number of members

   ii) High degree of complementarity and diversity of resources within the union.

   iii) High external tariff

   iv) Small cost difference of goods produced within the union

20) Primary goods are supply inelastic and income inelastic.

21) For stabilising export prices the following conditions should be present:-

   i)   Individual countries should have marketing boards.

   ii) Developing countries should jointly have international commodity agreements in export controls, bufer stocks and purchase contracts.

22) An open economy should maintain the following:-

   i)   Full employment

   ii) Economic growth

   iii) Internal equilibrium in price stability

   iv) External equilibrium in balance of payments and total currency flow at the prevailing exchange rate

23) The following are the determinants of the demand for a country' s currency:-

   i)   Foreign investors who wish to purchase the countrys stocks, bonds and other financial instruments.

   ii) Foreign companies which want to invest in the country.

   iii) Speculators who anticipate a decline in the value of foreign currencies relative to the local currency.

   iv) Firms, households or governments that import the countrys goods.

   v)   Foreign visitors travelling in the country.

24) The following are the determinants of the demand for a foreign countrys currency:-

   i)   Companies in the country which want to invest overseas.

   ii) Speculators who anticipate a rise in the value of foreign currencies relative to the country's currency.

   iii) Firms, households or governments that import foreign goods into the country.

   iv) Holders of local currency who wish to purchase foreign stocks, bonds and other financial instruments.

   v)   Citizens of the country travelling abroad.

25) The market forces that cause shifts in the supply and demand for a country's currency and hence its value are as follows:-

   i)   Changes in product availability whereby if country A suffers a bad crop failure, it would have to increase its food imports from country B. The demand for country B's exports and currency would increase so that its currency would appreciate in value.

   ii)   Relative interest rates changes whereby if interest rates rise in country A, people in country B would want to move their deposits to country A. The demand for country A's currency would rise and its currency would appreciate in value.

   iii)   Speculation takes place if speculators anticipate an increase in the price of country A's currency for one reason or another They would begin purchasing it, therefore pushing its price up. Country   A's currency would appreciate in value.

   iv)   Relative income changes whereby if incomes are rising more rapidly in country A than in country B, consumers in country A would tend to spend more, therefore increasing the demand for country B'   s exports and currency. Country B'currency would appreciate in value.

   v)   Relative price changes whereby if domestic prices are rising rapidly in country A, consumers in country A would seek out lower priced imports from country B. The demand for country B' s exports and currency would rise. Country B's currency would appreciate in value.

26) There used to be a fixed exchange rate system. But there has been a switch to a floating exchange rate system in 1973, whence the terminology used has also changed.

27) The terminology used for the two systems is as follows:-

   i)   Fixed exchange rate system: devaluation, revaluation

   ii)   Floating exchange rate system: depreciation, appreciation

28) The following are the different types of balances taken into consideration under the balance of payments:-

   i)   Capital account balance (inflows and outflows of capital)

   ii)   Merchandise trade balance (balance of exports and imports of goods)

   iii)   Service trade balance (balance of exports and imports of services)

   iv)   Current account balance (consisting of merchandise trade balance, service trade balance and unilateral transfers)

   v)   Overall balance (consisting of capital account balance, current account balance and errors and omissions of balancing)

29) When a country exports more than it imports it is said to have a favourable balance of trade while an unfavourable balance of trade means it imports more than it exports.

51. MONEY AND PRICE LEVEL

1) The following are the functions of money:-
   i) As a unit of account
   ii) As a medium of exchange
   iii) As a store of value
   iv) As a standard of deferred payment

2) Value of money = Quantity of goods and services which can be bought with a given sum of money

3) Price index = Means for measuring changes in the value of money = Weighted average of the price movements of a selected basket of commodities over a period of time

4) Monetary aggregates are quantitative measures of the supply of money and comprise the following:-
   i) Narrow money (or M1) consisting of currency in circulation and demand deposits or checking accounts.
   ii) Broad money (or M2) consisting of M1 plus other forms of deposits with other financial institutions.
   iii) Even broader definitions of money such as M3 include assets that are items or claims held on others that can be turned into cash or money.

5) The broader the definition of money the less liquid the money becomes.

6) The following are two other technical terms of money:-
   i) "Fiat money" - coins and paper currency decreed as legal tender and that must be accepted for private and public transactions, including repayment of debts. Not backed by gold and is not convertible into any commodity. Circulates on faith alone.
   ii) "Fiduciary issue" - the issue of currency not backed by gold (No currency in the world today is backed by gold)

7) The supply of money is fixed by the central bank or monetary authority.

8) The process of money creation as a result of the concept of fractional reserves allows monetry policy to be used for macroeconomic stabilisation.

9) Money creation or destruction depends on the money multiplier.

10) Money multiplier $= \dfrac{1}{\text{reserve requirement ratio}}$

11) The following are traditional functions of a central bank:-
   i) Issue money

ii)   Be the financial agent and banker to the government

iii) Be the lender of last resort to financial institutions

iv)   Ensure discipline and standards in the financial system

12) Demand for money = Derived demand for transactions and asset purposes

13) The determinants of the demand for money are as follows:-

i)   The level of transactions or GNP

ii)   The rate of interest

iii) The mode and frequency of payment

iv)   The availability of credit or charge cards

v)   Lifestyle

vi)   Portfolio balance

14) There are three motives for holding money (according to the Keynesian demand function or the liquidity preference theory):-

i)   Money is demanded as a medium of exchange for transactions. Demand for money is directly related to income and frequency and mode of payment.

ii)   Money is demanded too for spending at times of unforeseen emergencies.

iii) Money is demanded for speculation as a hedge against uncertainty.

15) The following four equations describe the quantity of money:-

i) $Md = kPT$

ii) $Ms = M$

iii) $Md = Ms$

iv) $M = kPT$

where: Md = Demand for money

Ms = Supply of money

M = Quantity of money

k = Constant

P = Price level

T = Volume of transactions

PT = Price level x Volume of transactions = Value of transactions

$Md = Ms$ = Equilibrium, whereby the money demanded equals the money supplied

16) The quantity theory of money presented as the equation of exchange is as follows:-

$MV = PT$

where: M = Quantity of money

V = Velocity of circulation of each unit of money

P = Price level

T = Volume of transactions

PT = Price level x Volume of transactions = Money value of total output = Nominal GDP

17) The four instruments of monetary policy are as follows:-

i) Required reserve ratio

ii) Discount rate

iii) Open market operations

iv) Moral suasion

52. NATIONAL INCOME ACCOUNTING

1) Possible problems in computing a country's national income:-

a) Nominal versus real prices in inter-temporal comparisons.

b) International comparisons for different countries at the same point in time may be difficult as national currencies have to be converted to a common currency, e.g., the US dollar, for comparability.

c) Conceptual differences in the definitions of national output or income, e.g., in the centrally planned economies as against the market economies.

d) Different levels of statistical coverage and consistency between developed and developing countries which may afect accuracy and therefore comparability of their national output.

2) Basis of all national income computations is simple circular flow between households and firms.

3) This can be made more realistic and therefore more complicated by adding the following:-

a) Withdrawals comprising saving, imports and taxes.

b) Injections making up of investment, exports and government expenditure.

4) Gross National Product (GNP) or Gross Domestic Product (GDP) includes the following:-

a) Market transactions and economic production, e.g., in manufacturing and service sectors.

b) Imputed income or payments-in-kind, e.g., rent on owner-occupied housing.

But excludes the following:-

a)   Intermediate goods, used assets, and, stocks and bonds.

b)   Illegal activities such as smuggling, gambling, drugs and prostitution.

c)   Domestic production (services of housewives) and all do-it-yourself work.

d)   Environmental harm and other disamenities.

e)   Leisure activities which increase value and utility.

5)   GNP or GDP is normally used as indicator of level of development and welfare in a country.

6)   It is strictly a measure of production only.

7)   It is hampered by conceptual and statistical limitations.

8)   The Measure of Welfare (MEW) is better than the GNP or GDP in measuring the level of development and welfare of a country as it comprises items pertaining to welfare, which are not included in the GNP or GDP.

9)   MEW = NNP + Leisure Activity + Underground Activity - Pollution and Disamenity.

53. THE ECONOMIC ROLE OF GOVERNMENT

1)   Role of government in economy is fundamentally a principal-agent relationship which arises because of the following factors:-

i)   Asymmetry of information whereby one party has more information.

ii)   Necessity of delegating many critical tasks to another party.

2)   The following are the possible causes of problems:-

i)   The ballot box is a crude indicator of public satisfaction and an ineffective mechanism for controlling the management of state activities.

ii)   Principals do not know whether their agents are serving their interests faithfully and efficiently.

iii)   Agents may misuse, neglect or even act against principals' interests for their own selfish motives.

3)   The following are three traditional functions of the government:-

i)   Attain desirable rate of economic growth with full employment of resources and stable price levels.

ii)   Ensure efficiency in allocation of resources.

iii)   Achieve equitable distribution of income.

4) The reasons for government intervention are as follows:-

    i) External factors which coerce the government to act for the sake of public good.

    ii) The necessary provision of public goods and merit goods for the benefit of every citizen.

    iii) The government has the responsibility and concern for public welfare.

5) The government can be of any size.

6) The roles and functions of government vary from country to country.

7) Its roles and functions depend on the country's stage of development and its ideology.

8) The following are the usual indicators of the size of a government:-

    i) The number of jobs provided by the government.

    ii) The government's contribution to the economy.

    iii) The ratio of government expenditure to GDP.

    iv) The ratio of government revenue to GDP.

    v) The ratio of total government budget (expenditure and revenue) to GDP.

9) The government influences the economy through the following:-

    i) Monetary policies pertaining to the regulation of money supply.

    ii) Fiscal policies, e.g., increasing or lowering taxes and increasing or decreasing spending on public works.

10) The various aspects of taxation are as follows:-

    i) Types of taxes (direct and indirect).

    ii) Effect of taxation (progressive, proportional and regressive).

    iii) Bases of taxation (income, wealth and consumption/expenditure).

    iv) Principles of implementation of taxation (public's ability to pay and public benefit).

11) The following are some possible results of government intervention:-

    i) Conflicts of policy between economic growth, income distribution and fairness.

    ii) Bureaucratic red tape, inefficiencies or corruption within the government.

    iii) Disparity between political need to serve the public and government inefficiency.

54. THE THEORY OF NATIONAL INCOME DETERMINATION

1) The main theories behind national income determination are the Classical and Keynesian schools of thought.

2) The Classical school assumes:-

   i) Full employment of resources

   ii) Perfectly competitive markets

   iii) Flexible interest rates, prices and wages

   iv) Say's law (which states that supply creates its own demand)

   v) A vertical aggregate supply in the long run

   vi) Free market policy

   vii) Individuals are self-motivated

   viii) No money illusion

3) The Keynesian school assumes:-

   i) Unemloyment of resources

   ii) Prices, especially wages, are not flexible downwards

   iii) Saving and investment are necessarily equal as investment is not sensitive to interest rate

   iv) The government plays an important part in the kind of fiscal policy it implements

   v) The aggregate supply is more elastic

4) In its simplest form, national income could be expressed through the following equation:-

   National Income = National Output = National Expenditure

   where: National Income represents the incomes of all the citizens

   National Output represents the creation of wealth by the nations industries

   National Expenditure represents what we spend or lend to the banks who invest it

5) According to Alfred Marshall, national income is "the aggregate net product of, and the sole source of payment for , all the agents of production".

6) Measuring the national income allows us to control the economy and obtain the maximum economic benefit from it.

7) The following are the three methods of measuring national income:-

   i) Total-factor-incomes method

ii) Aggregate-net-production method

iii) Total-national-expenditure method

8) When using any of these three methods to measure national income, care should be exercised in order to avoid double-counting.

9) There should be clear definitions of the measurements to be made, which have to be borne in mind when using or interpreting the data.

10) According to the Keynesian model of income determination, the aggregate monetary demand (AD) consists of the following:-

i) Consumption function (C)

ii) Investment function (I)

iii) Government function (G)

iv) Export function (X)

v) Import function (M)

11) For a closed economy, aggregate monetary demand = consumption plus investment plus government expenditure. (AD = C + I + G)

12) For an open economy, aggregate monetary demand = consumption plus investment plus government expenditure plus exports minus imports, exports minus imports being net exports. (AD = C + I + G + (X - M))

13) The consumption function, which is important, consists of the following:-

i) An autonomous (and exogenous) part that is independent of income (whether the consumers earn an income or not they have to consume).

ii) An induced (and endogenous) part which changes with the changes in the level of income and the marginal propensity to consume.

14) Marginal propensity to consume = $\dfrac{\text{Change in consumption}}{\text{Change in income}}$

15) Average propensity to consume = $\dfrac{\text{Total consumption}}{\text{Total income}}$

16) The consumption function (C) could be expressed through the following equation:-

C = a + bY

where: a = Autonomous consumption

b = Marginal propensity to consume

Y = Income

17) An increase in the aggregate level of consumption results in an increase in the aggregate demand, all things being equal. An increase in consumption could also give rise to an increase in imports and trade imbalance, with the trade imbalance leading to problems in the balance of payments and foreign exchange rates.

18) The interaction between aggregate demand, national income and level of employment affects the economy, i.e., inflation or deflation could result.

19) Investment = Net addition to the economy's capital stock = Real capital formation

20) Investment is a "flow" variable, which could be autonomous or induced.

21) Autonomous investment, known as capital investment, e.g., houses and roads, is independent of the national income level (income inelastic), and depends more on population growth and technological progress, and are often undertaken by the government in anticipation of population growth, technological demands, etc..

22) Induced investment is affected by the changes in national income, which would bring about changes in the aggregate demand, which would in turn affect the volume of investment.

23) This kind of investment is income elastic, i.e., it increases as income increases and vice versa.

24) Induced investment is made in fixed capital and inventories in anticipation of rising demands.

25) Changes in the prices of goods and factors, interest rates and profit level affect induced investment.

26) The following are the main determinants of investment:-
   i)   Marginal efficiency of capital (MEC)
   ii)   Income level
   iii) Interest rate
   iv)   Multiplier and accelerator value
   v)   Technological change, etc.

27) Investment brings about great economic activities; it creates employment and raises the income of the factors of production, which in turn stimulates demand and results in increased output to meet this increased demand. The effect of an increase in investment on national income is dependent on the value of the multiplier -accelerator, the greater the value of the multiplier-accelerator, the greater would be the increase in national income.

28) Marginal efficiency of capital (MEC) - it is the yield accruing from an additional unit of capital; if interest rate is low there would be more investment and vice versa; an increase in the MEC would result in more investment at every rate of interest; fluctuations in the MEC would result in fluctuations in investment.

29) The MEC could be described as a firm's annual earnings from funds invested in a capital good, expressed as a percentage of the funds invested, i.e., it is the highest expected rate of return (profit) likely to be obtained

from a marginal increase in the rate of investment, as demonstrated by the following equation:-

$$MEC = \frac{\text{Expected Returns (Profits)}}{\text{Initial Cost}} \times 100\%$$

30) National income level - a higher level of national income would give rise to a greater demand for goods and services, which would in turn lead to more investment and increased production.

31) Interest rates - low interest rates mean that borrowing costs are low; lower borrowing costs encourage more bank loans, which mean more investment; an interest rate is the price paid for a loan, the price for parting with liquidity, and could be determined through the demand for real capital and the supply of savings (as stipulated by the classical theory) and through the demand for and supply of money balances (as stipulated by the Keynesian theory); cutting the interest rates would affect investments and the national income; investment decisions depend on the interest rate and the marginal efficiency of capital (MEC).

32) Multiplier and accelerator value - the multiplier is the ratio of the change in national income to an initial change in expenditure which brought it about, it is the number of times by which the changes in injection have to be multiplied to obtain the resulting change in national income; the accelerator principle stipulates that an increase in national income would lead to an increase in the demand for investment goods and that a relatively small increase in national income would result in a greater increase in the demand for investment or capital goods; the interacting of both the multiplier and the accelerator would produce a greater effect; the following are the equations for the investment multiplier and the accelerator:-

i)   Investment Multiplier (k) = $\dfrac{\text{Change in Output or National Income}}{\text{Change in Investment}}$

ii)   Accelerator (a) = $\dfrac{\text{Change in Investment}}{\text{Change in National Income}}$

33) Technological change - there is a need for firms to invest in the capital goods which have the latest technology so that they would not lose out to their competitors, which would mean more investment.

34) Government function - represents government expenditure (net) of taxation, is assumed to be autonomous since it is politically motivated, government expenditure would result in an increase in the national income, government expenditure generally does not depend on the interest rate but depends on the macroeconomic, political and social policies.

35) Net exports - they are the exports minus the imports; exports bring income into the country while imports result in money flowing out of the country; exports depend on foreigners' level of income whereas imports depend on the domestic income, and, the mar ginal propensity to import whose equation is as follows:-

$$\text{Marginal propensity to import} = \frac{\text{Change in import}}{\text{Change in income}}$$

36) The level of national income would be in equilibrium when all the variables in the economy are equal, when all injections (additions to the circular flow of income) are equal to all withdrawals.

37) The circular flow of income represents the flow of income from economic agent to economic agent; the flow of income comprises of real and monetary flow; real flow represents the flow of factor services and goods and services; monetary flow represents the flow of money i.e., payments for factor services and expenditures on goods and services; production gives rise to income and income gives rise to expenditure; the circular flow of income would go on indefinitely if households spend all the incomes they earn from selling their factor services and if firms pay the households all the payments they get from the sales of their production; in real life this would not happen since there are injections into and withdrawals from the flow of income, which changes all the time.

38) Injections are the additions to the circular flow of income; they consist of the incomes earned by domestic firms which do not arise out of the expenditure of domestic households and the incomes earned by households which do not arise out of the expenditure of domestic firms; they put expansionary pressure on the economy; they (J) are assumed to be autonomous and consist of the following:-

i) Government expenditure (G) - government expenditure on projects that creates income which does not arise out of the spending of households and the activities of firms.

ii) Investments (I) - they represent spending on goods and services which are not for present consumption but for expansion of the productive capacity and might be financed by past savings or borrowings from households or financial institutions.

iii)   Exports   (X) - they are domestic goods and
                                       services which are sold abroad,
                                       resulting in money flowing into the
                                       country.

39) Withdrawals are those incomes that are not passed on into the circular
     flow and are thus not available for spending on goods and services that
     are currently produced; they exercise contractionary pressure on the
     economy; they vary with income and the higher the level of income the
     greater these withdrawals would be; there is equilibrium in the circular
     flow of income when all injections are equal to all withdrawals; they (W)
     consist of the following:-

     i)   Savings (S) - unspent incomes/savings of households and firms

     ii)   Taxes   (T) - payments made to the tax authority

     iii) Imports (M) - goods and services brought into the country ,
                          resulting in money flowing out of the country

40) In an open economy which has a government sector, there is equilibrium
     when: government expenditure plus investments plus exports equal
     savings plus taxes plus imports $(G + I + X = S + T + M)$, i.e., injections
     equal withdrawals $(J = W)$.

41) The multiplier (k), being the number of times by which a change in
     injection has to be multiplied to get the resulting change in national income,
     could be described by the following equations:-

$$\text{Multiplier (k)} = \frac{\text{Change in National Income}}{\text{Change in Injection}}$$

$$= \frac{\text{Change in National Income}}{\text{Change in Withdrawal}}$$

(when there is an equilibrium, i.e., Injection =
Withdrawal $(J = W)$)

$$= \frac{1}{\text{Marginal Propensity to Withdraw}}$$

(as Marginal Propensity to Withdraw (MPW) = Change
in Withrawal divided by Change in National Income)

$$= \frac{1}{MPS + MTR + MPM}$$

(as Withdrawal (W) = Savings (S) +Taxes (T) + Imports
(M), and, Marginal Propensity to Withdraw (MPW) =

Marginal Propensity to Save (MPS) + Maginal Tax Rate (MTR) + Marginal Propensity to Import (MPM))

$$= \frac{1}{MPS} \quad \text{(for a closed economy)}$$

42) The Keynesian model of national income determination is based on the following assumptions:-

i) The presence of massive unemployment.

ii) The stability of wages and factor prices.

iii) Though aggregate demand, output and employment level might increase, wages and factor prices would be unchanged.

iv) The techniques of production remain the same.

v) The potential national income, which corresponds to the full employment level of all resources in the economy , remains unchanged.

43) The following are the three approaches which could be used to determine the equilibrium level of national income:-

i) Income-expenditure approach

ii) Savings-investment approach

iii) Withdrawal-injection approach

55. MONEY AND FINANCIAL MARKETS

1) Money serves the following four specific functions: medium of exchange, unit of account, store of value and standard of deferred payment.

2) The supply of money is regulated by each country's monetary authority, i.e., the central bank or federal reserve, whose monetary policy focuses on maintaining a sound financial system in which people have confidence.

3) The money supply in a country is increased or decreased mainly through open-market operations.

4) The other way of increasing or decreasing the country's money supply is through the required reserve ratio.

5) Money is created by the banking system according to the money multiplier relationship between deposits, the required reserve ratio and loans offered by banks.

6) The demand for liquid money could be described as transactions, precautions and speculative demands (motives for holding money).

7) Interest rates in the money market are determined by money supply and money demand.

8) The real interest rate is the dif ference between the nominal rate and inflation.

9) Both the nominal and real interest rates are taken into consideration for consumption, saving and investment decisions.

10) They therefore affect aggregate demand.

11) The quantity theory of money describes the relationship between money supply and inflation.

12) Inflation expectations also play a part in the determination of ex-ante real interest rates used for decision-making.

13) The stability of a country's financial system depends on the credibility of the central bank policies.

14) The exchange rates in the foreign exchange market are determined by the currency supply and demand.

15) The speculation in money and other asset markets is widespread in the economy.

16) Speculation involves costs and benefits.

17) The monetary policy could focus on a number of targets.

18) Monetary policy is the broad term which is used to describe how the money supply is regulated in an economy , including how inflation is controlled and how the currency's stability is maintained.

19) When the central bank buys or sells government bonds it carries out an open-market operation.

20) A bond is an agreement between two parties in a transaction wherein one party lends money to the other for an agreed interest rate over a specific period of time, and, the lender gets back the total value of their investment when the bond matures.

21) The demand for bonds is dependent on their rate of return or interest.

22) Government bonds are issued to generate funds for the government, usually maturing after ten years or more.

23) Purchasers of bonds pay money in return for an agreed rate of return on their investment in the future.

24) The central bank increases the money supply by buying government bonds from the public thus releasing an additional supply of money.

25) The central bank could sell some of its own reserves of government bonds, therefore taking money out of circulation and transferring it into its reserves, if it wanted to reduce the money supply.

26) To compare the future receipt of a bond with a current receipt of the same value requires a method for comparing benefits in different time periods which is known as the present value determination.

27) The following is the standard formula which is used to determine present value:-

$$PV = \frac{£X}{(1+r)^T}$$

where: PV represents present value

$£X$ is the amount to be received in the future

r is the market interest rate

T is the number of years before the investment is repaid

28) The present value increases as the period of the investment declines because of people's preference for 1 today rather than one year,two years, etc., from the present.

29) A lower interest rate increases the present value of a bond.

30) The required reserve ratio is the percentage of all deposits received by banks which have to be held in the bank and not used for loans or other purposes.

31) As banks have to hold a fraction of their deposits in the form of reserves, the banking system is known as a fractional reserve system.

32) The money multiplier describes how a change in money supply leads to an ultimate change in the supply of money by a multiple of the initial change.

33) The size of the multiplier varies with the required reserve ratio according to the following formula:-

$$\text{Money Multiplier} = \frac{1}{\text{Required Reserve Ratio}}$$

34) The real interest rate (r) is computed as the difference between the nominal interest rate and rate of inflation as follows:-

$r = i - \pi$

where: i denotes the nominal rate and π represents the rate of inflation

35) A change in the aggregate price level is caused by a change in money supply.

36) An increase in the price level is called inflation.

37) Therefore, inflation is caused by increasing the supply of money.

38) Thus, a change in the supply of money results in the same proportional change in the aggregate price level, if real output is regarded as constant.

39) Inflation = Rate of money supply growth - Rate of real output growth

E.g., inflation = 10% - 6% = 4%

40) A central bank has limited control of the interest rate in the short run.

41) Independence from the government is important for central bank credibility - independence means that the government has no direct input into the economic decisions made by the central bank regarding money supply , interest rates and inflation.

42) The Taylor rules describe how interest rates are set by a central bank, a general form of which is as follows:-

Nominal interest rate = Equilibrium nominal interest rate +A percentage of the output gap + A percentage of the inflation gap

43) Changes in inflation expectations could change the outcome which is predicted by the money demand and supply model.

44) The price of one currency in terms of another currency is known as the exchange rate.

45) An appreciation of a currency occurs when a unit of it buys more foreign currency today than it did yesterday i.e., it costs more in terms of foreign currency to buy it.

46) A depreciation of a currency occurs when a unit of it buys less foreign currency today than it did yesterday, i.e., it costs less in terms of foreign currency to purchase it.

47) The changes in exchange rates are caused by the following main factors:-
   i)   Interest rate differentials
   ii)   Inflation differentials
   iii)   Growth differentials
   iv)   Speculation

48) Arbitrage refers to the possibility of buying an asset, e.g., foreign exchange, in one market and selling it at a higher price in another market.

49) In the futures markets, agreements are made relating to a payment which would be made for the delivery of goods in the future.

50) In the spot or cash markets, money changes hands today for the goods or services received today.

51) Debt financing results in the borrowing of money which must usually be repaid with interest.

52) Equity financing involves selling a share of the business in exchange for finance, without the specific future payment defined.

53) The real value of the fixed-income investment is reduced when inflation is greater than the rate of return.

54) Exchange rates which are determined by demand and supply are known as floating exchange rates.

55) If a country's exchange rate is tied to another country's rate, it is known as a fixed exchange rate.

56) There are many signs which indicate that economies are becoming more interdependent.

57) The optimal currency area (OCA) theory identifies the factors which determine whether a single currency maximizes single-currency benefits for the countries with economic links, given the costs generated.

58) The following four factors play a central role in the determination of the success or failure of any common currency:-

    i)   Extent of trade with currency partners

    ii) Effect of economic shocks vis-à-vis currency partners

    iii) Extent of labour mobility between currency partners

    iv) Extent of fiscal transfers between currency partners

59) Realignments are simultaneous and coordinated devaluation or revaluation of the currencies of several countries.

60) The balance of payments is one account in a country's national accounts, consisting of a current account and a capital account.

61) It includes transactions between domestic residents and the rest of the world over a specific period of time.

56. ECONOMIC ACTIVITIES IN GENERAL

Definitions Of Business

1) A business is a commercial or industrial establishment.

2) A business is a collection of people or resources involved in providing goods or services for an end user or customer.

Business Activities

1) The aim of a business is to make a profit - the money earned or received by the business should be more than the money paid out.

2) If the business makes a profit it could grow.

3) If it makes a loss it might have to borrow money from a bank.

4) For business activities to take place, money is needed.

5) The businessman has to take risks.

6) The business has to satisfy the needs of customers (physiological needs, security needs, social needs, status needs and self actualisation needs).

7) A business has to combine the various different inputs (resources) to produce an output for its customers.

8) The business incurs opportunity cost - the money they invest in the business could not be used for other purposes.

9) The business has to add value to a product so that the customer would desire the product.

10) The business has to be aware of the external forces which might encourage or hinder its success and growth.

11) The customer's support is very important to the business; the business has to pay close attention to the customer and ensure that he is satisfied with the product or service provided by the business.

12) The business has to realise that the customer is always demanding for more and better products or services.

13) The business sells its products in the market, e.g., the shop, the showroom or the internet. (A market is a place where buyers meet sellers.)

Types Of Products

1) Fast Moving Consumer Goods (fmcgs)

These are consumer non-durables which are sold to consumers, week in, week out, which are consumed only once, e.g., all food products, shampoo, dog biscuits, etc.. Such products are frequently purchased.

2) Consumer Durables

These products are purchased less frequently by consumers and could be used many times, e.g., cars, washing machines and carpets.

3) Capital Goods

These are products supplied by one business to anothere.g., components, fork-lift trucks, cranes and welding equipment.

Inputs And Outputs Of Business

1) The inputs are the resources a business puts in.

2) The inputs are also known as factors of production - land, labour, capital (and materials) and managerial ability (enterprise).

Land

Land is any asset on, under and above the ground, e.g., farm land and the land on which a multi-storey industrial building stands.

Labour

Labour comprises the skill and ef fort people use at work, for which they are paid wages or salaries.

Capital

These are the things needed to operate the business, e.g., components, storage systems, vehicles, buildings, machinery, fuel and raw materials.

Managerial Ability

This is the ability to use resources efficiently so that the most output is obtained from the least input, which means that each unit of output is produced at the lowest cost.

Money

1) Money is the medium of exchange which customers use to pay for the products or services they purchase and which the business enterprises use to pay their suppliers.

2) Money could take the form of hard cash, cheques, transfers through bank accounts via a computer, credit cards or debit cards.

Business Functions

Marketing

1) Marketing involves the process which identifies customer needs and devises a strategy which would satisfy those needs.

2) This strategy involves the four Ps - product (quality and features), price (pricing strategies), place (of distribution) and promotion (e.g., advertising and personal selling).

Production (Operations)

1) Production is the process whereby inputs of people, machinery and materials are converted into outputs of finished goods or services, e.g., a factory manufacturing chocolate bars and the solicitor's clerk allocating cases, organising paperwork and ensuring that the solicitors have an organised, structured day (i.e., carrying out the day-to-day operations of the legal firm).

Finance

1) Finance is needed to pay staff salaries and purchase equipment and materials for the business.

2) The Finance department is involved in the careful planning of revenue and expenditure, i.e., budgeting.

3) Each department would be given a budget in terms of expenditure targets and, where appropriate, revenue targets.

4) The individual departmental budgets make up the total budget for th business.

5) Such a budget is sometimes used to persuade banks to provide loans and potential investors to invest in the business.

People (Human Resources)

1) All businesses involve people or require manpower.

2) The success of a business depends very frequently on the skill level, motivation and initiative of its staff.

3) The Personnel department or Human Resource Management department has the responsibility to select, train and organise the staff or employees according to the needs of each department.

4) The business should achieve the best from its staf f, from workers to managers and directors, so that the performance of the business might not suffer.

Directors

1) As the business expands, the managers become more involved in the day-to-day operations of the business, and the longer-term perspective might be ignored.

2) It is the director's responsibility to consider the long-term objectives of the business and to ensure that resources are or ganised carefully so that long-term objectives are achieved.

3) The directors report to and submit company reports to the shareholders of the business.

4) The directors are answerable to the shareholders of the business regarding the profitability of the business.

5) Although directors are not known as managers, their whole job is about management.

Management

1) Management is the process which involves the following activities:-

    i) Planning

    ii) Organising

    iii) Controlling

    iv) Co-ordinating

    v) Motivating

2) Management activities are divided into the various functions, e.g., marketing management, personnel management, financial management and production management, with individual managers in chage of each function whose task it is to ensure that the process of business activity is carried out according to the various objectives of the business.

Opportunity Cost

1) Opportunity cost is the cost of giving up the next best alternative when choosing one alternative.

2) The business has to consider the opportunity costs when making business decisions.

3) Investing money in a project might mean not being able to enjoy the benefits of investing money in another project.

Risk Versus Profit

1) There are many ways of investing one's money, e.g., put it in a bank to earn interest, invest it in a building society invest it in government bonds, use it to purchase shares in a safe, large business like McDonald's that is likely to grow steadily , invest it in a business that has launched a revolutionary new product, etc..

2) Some investments are riskier than others.

3) Normally, the riskier the investment is the higher the returns would be. (No pain, no gain. No venture, no gain.)

4) Business normally involves risks and people in business have to be prepared to take some risks. (Many people in business take calculated risks.)

Added Value

1) Every business should attempt to add value in everything it does.

2) Business decisions are evaluated according to the amount of added value which would result.

3) The more efficient businesses would try to get rid of all those processes which add costs without adding value.

4) Added value is normally earned by either making a production process more efficient, e.g., by eliminating waste, or, by encouraging customers through effective marketing to purchase a product at a price that is greater than the cost.

5) The end result is that the customer is willing to pay more for the product than the costs of producing it.

External Factors

1) A business might encounter problems which it would need to solve, e.g., staff leaving the company late delivery of materials and unskilled workers.

2) There are external forces which might provide opportunities for business growth or constrain the business.

3) These external forces are as follows:-

    i) Environment

    ii) Economic climate

    iii) Culture and purchasing habits

    iv) Unions

    v) Government

    vi) Competition

Manufacturing Versus Services

Business activity could be divided into the following four stages of production:-

1) Primary Sector

  i)   This sector is involved in the extraction or creation of raw materials.

  ii) This sector is dominant in countries with a wealth of raw materials or perhaps a wealth of rich, fertile land which could be used to grow crops.

  iii) The activities carried out in this sector include mining, e.g., gold and coal mining, farming or agriculture and animal husbandry e.g., rearing of cattle and sheep.

2) Secondary Sector

  i)   This sector is involved in manufacturing activities using the raw materials obtained from the primary sector , e.g., converting raw materials into part-finished goods or components and then assembling these part-finished goods or components.

3) Tertiary Sector

  i)   This sector comprises the services which have evolved from the success of manufacturing.

  ii) In Britain, this service sector is responsible for a significant part of economic growth.

  iii) This sector includes all the supporting services, e.g., financial services provided by banks and building societies, and, services provided by estate agents, retailers, accountants, solicitors, recruitment agencies, cleaners, etc..

4) Quaternary Sector

  i)   This sector has evolved in recent years, based on the revolution in IT.

  ii) This sector includes IT support services, internet services and computer technology upgrading services.

Importance Of Manufacturing

1) Business activity depends much on manufacturing.

2) If there is no manufacturing, the country has to import or buy goods from abroad.

3) Manufacturing has declined much in recent years; in Britain, manufacturing has been replaced by an increase in the service industry.

4) Services could exist only if manufacturing exists, e.g., loans for houses could not be granted unless the houses have been built in the first place and shops require the manufactured goods to sell.

5) It is better to manufacture the goods than to import the goods from another country.

6) Importing the goods from another country means that money is leaving our country for the country from which the goods are imported, making that country wealthier at our expense.

57. ECONOMIC ACTIVITIES AND THE ENVIRONMENT

The Context Of Business

1) Whenever a business considers a decision which costs money and takes time to implement, it has to take into account many external factors over which it has no control.

2) There are many factors which influence a company's success.

3) The business has to be able to judge which factors are the most important and to what extent each of them would influence the business.

4) To survive, the business has to react in an appropriate way.

5) The following external factors could influence a business:-
   i) Competition
   ii) European Union
   iii) Law
   iv) Economic issues
   v) Political influence
   vi) Customer bias
   vii) Social issues
   ix) Environmental issues
   x) Culture
   xi) Pressure groups
   xii) Ethics
   xiii) Technological change

6) The largest companies, e.g., Microsoft, which has to compete carefully with Apple, a much smaller company whose products are reputedly more powerful and more useful in certain circumstances, are also influenced by such factors.

7) A large and wealthy company such as Microsoft, attracts much unwanted media attention.

8) Large companies are sometimes able to influence other companies in their decision-making.

9) The smaller companies, e.g.,Apple, have to react to the lager companies', e.g., Microsoft's great influence in the market.

The External Forces Considered

(Acronym for helping to remember the external factors: SELECT CCEEPP)

Social

1) Decisions made by companies are often influenced by the structure of the population, e.g., changes in the population structure, which are known as demographic trends.

2) Demographic trends constitute a much more complicated shift from young to old markets.

3) For example, customers nowadays are wealthier, more health-conscious, more thoughtful and careful when selecting products.

4) This means that manufacturers would have to improve their designs and be flexible in their production to meet customers' needs.

5) Customers might, e.g., on account of their affluence, invest more in homes, and, home prices would increase, which would be reflected in the level of money being passed on in inheritance.

6) As health care is more advanced, people are living longer , a fact which businesses should note.

Economic

1) Businesses are affected by the local, national and international economy.

2) How much businesses are affected would depend on how widely spread the business is across the world and how much it depends on one market/economy/product.

3) An economic crisis in a region, e.g., South-East-Asia, would afect many companies.

4) For example, many western companies who had property manufacturing plants or customers in South-East-Asia were affected by the Asian crisis of 1997 and 1998.

5) The affected companies could then make an attempt to remove their investment from the region as quickly as possible.

Legal

1) Planning permission from the authorities would be required in certain business activities, e.g., converting a garage into a place of residence.

2) Failure to obtain planning permission for such a conversion would result in loss of revenue for the builders.

3) Other government regulations which affect businesses and customers are the laws on employment contracts, the Health and Safety aWork Act and the Sale of Goods Act.

Environment

1) Though consumers expect companies to be responsible for protecting the

environment while carrying out their activities, companies are likely to do so if it means extra revenue, but not if it means extra costs.

2) It is only the fear of penalties from the government which prompts companies to spend money on environmental protection.

3) For example, the Environment Protection Agency in Britain imposed a 1 billion fine on diesel truck engine makers in 1998 for contravening clean air regulations.

Customer Base

1) A customer base is the set of customers who purchase products from companies.

2) There would be a problem for the business if there is a change in the customer base (as customers change their demands and lifestyles).

3) As markets have become more segmented and consumers' income has risen, this has become more significant.

4) Therefore, businesses have to be flexible and able to react to any changes.

5) As the characteristics of the population change, businesses have to adapt to meet the needs of consumers.

6) For example, the customer base of BT mobile phones, which used to be businessmen and women, due to the change in trends, now includes a much wider section of the population.

Technology

1) Technological change is one of the most important, and at times, frightening, aspects of our lives.

2) It has resulted in the reduction of workers, who are replaced by machines.

3) More information needs to be processed than ever before and as technology changes very quickly technical products, e.g., photocopiers, have a much shorter shelf life.

4) Photocopiers, e.g., are now cheaper to hire, produce better quality reproductions and can produce them at a speed of nearly 100 per minute.

5) As the demand from customers for faster machines becomes greater new products are frequently produced.

Competition

1) Most businesses have competitors, except for monopolies.

2) Some companies, e.g., those supplying water, electricity and gas, might have faced no competition at the initial stage, though the competition came later.

3) Some industries are highly concentrated, i.e., a lar ge proportion of the total market is controlled by relatively few companies, e.g., in food retailing where six or seven lar ge companies could take up more than

50% of the total market while thousands of other companies compete for the rest. (This is an oligopoly.)

4) When the number of companies increases and no individual company is able to exert control over the market, competition would become fiercer

5) For example, companies which supply windows and doors do more or less the same thing, sell rather similar products from the same manufacturer and therefore have to work very hard to stay competitive.

Culture

1) An increase in the number of immigrants and the dif   ferences in their cultures, e.g., religious beliefs, ethical beliefs and work attitudes, bring new opportunities to businesses.

2) For example, more women now join the work-force, fuelling the growth in child-care services and play groups, and, the employment of more nannies and au pairs.

3) Companies such as Land Rover now provide crèche facilities as their female employees work longer hours.

Ethics

1) Business ethics is much more than issues such as human rights and testing products on humans and animals.

2) It could involve anything ranging from the payment of wages, the way the business is managed, promptness of payments to suppliers, aids to the community or some charitable causes and purchasing products from countries where there is exploitation of labour.

3) Corporate governance involves the way a business is or ganised, and, in particular, how the directors run the business.

4) For example, the annual report of BOC (British Oxygen Group) states that it has more plants producing gas which are certified to ISO 14001 than any other industrial gas company.

Europe

1) The introduction of the euro (a currency) is perhaps the most important part of the influence exerted from Europe.

2) Since the Single Market was established in 1992, there have been several thousand European Community directives over a wide range of industries, e.g., consistent quality standards for manufacturing across the European Union.

3) Such standardisation means that a product made within the European Union could be used anywhere within the Union, e.g., a plug produced within th Union would fit the plug points in Portugal, France and Spain.

Political

1) Political objectives could result in the government introducing laws such as the minimum wage, which would ensure that employees or workers have a more decent standard of living.

2) Companies already paying their workers above the minimum wage could feel pressured to increase their workers' wages so that the latter would not feel that they lost out.

3) This would increase the costs of such companies.

Pressure Groups

1) Pressure groups could greatly influence the way a business operates, e.g., unions could influence wage rates across entire industries and cause inconvenience to customers by organising strikes.

2) Other pressure groups such as consumer af fairs magazines could bring serious media attention to companies which do not provide adequate customer service.

58. ECONOMIC ACTIVITIES: MARKETING AND DEMOGRAPHY

What Is Marketing?

1) Chartered Institute of Marketing's Definition Of Marketing: Marketing is the "identification, anticipation and satisfaction of the customer's needs, profitably".

2) Marketing is frequently confused with advertising or publicity stunts - a far too narrow definition.

3) Marketing is wider than just advertising and publicity.

4) Another definition of marketing: Getting the right product to the right customers at the right price at the right time.

5) This implies that marketing involves a range of activities, which has to achieve all of the following:-

   i) Market products which the customer demands.

   ii) Fix a price which the customer could afford.

   iii) Distribute the product to a place where the customer would purchase it.

   iv) Carry out promotion to persuade the customer to purchase in a competitive market.

6) The above involves the four Ps - Product, Price, Place (Distribution) and Promotion, which could be referred to as the marketing mix.

7) Though the business could use the four Ps to satisfy the consumer , they would still need to make a profit in order to survive.

From Product To Market Orientation

1) Instead of relying on competitive advantage, producers have been simply developing products which they thought would sell.

2) They then used hard-selling advertising and an aggressive sales-force to generate sales.

3) This was a "hit or miss" approach and the producers could be left with lots of unsold stock.

4) This was known as product orientation.

5) Some companies were successful in using this approach.

6) For example, Sir Clive Sinclair developed and marketed the pocket calculator without having carried out any market research, but merely anticipated the demand for the product, and was highly successful, until a larger, more efficient company, Casio, began to compete.

7) His second product, the C5, was also produced and marketed without any market research but was a failure.

8) The other approach is known as market orientation.

9) In this approach, the needs of the customer are assessed through the use of market research.

10) After market research, the company would develop a product that fits those needs and that could be sold at a profit.

Growth Of Marketing

It is only recently that companies begin to place more emphasis on marketing.

Mass Production

1) Mass production implies that products are manufactured in anticipation of demand, and not what customers actually want.

2) Henry Ford, an automobile pioneer , was able to manufacture his Ford cars so efficiently, relying on economies of scale, that the cars became significantly reduced in price.

3) Low price was the unique selling point (USP) of the Ford car - it distinguished the Ford car from others.

Economic Growth

1) After the Second World War, governments all over the world invested heavily in rebuilding the infrastructure of their countries.

2) This created new-found wealth. People earned more money and thus had more money to spend.

3) They were able to buy higher-quality products.

4) Companies which produced these products to meet demand were highly profitable.

5) This attracted more companies into the market.

6) The consumer was thus given greater choice.

Competition

1) Competition would coerce companies to try and dif ferentiate themselves from each other.

2) Each of these companies would have to find out what their customers want, develop a unique selling point and sell products which are diErent from th rest.

Technology

1) Sophisticated data collection and storage methods have enabled companies to anticipate purchasing habits.

2) The technology of the equipment utilised to manufacture products and the products themselves have become more technologically advanced.

3) Being able to have access to the stock of finished goods quickly and prompt deliveries to customers, e.g., next day deliveries, have become common.

4) For example, Japanese car manufacturers have made prompt delivery a standard practice.

Marketing Objectives

1) Marketing a product would be af fected by the objectives set by the company.

2) For example, survival might be the main objective of a new business, with the marketing objectives aligned to it.

3) It would be more important for a new company or a company introducing a new product to gain recognition in the market and establish a customer base.

4) For an established company, it might be more important for it to increase its market share by concentrating on establishing and extending brand loyalty, e.g., by getting existing customers to purchase more of the product or finding new customers.

5) Increasing the market share could enable the company to enjoy economies of scale, dominate the market and possibly prevent other companies from joining the market, and, charge a range of prices for the same product in different market segments (price discrimination).

6) A marketing objective could also involve reducing the demand for a particular product or activity , e.g., government advertisements prior to the Christmas season warning people of the hazards of drinking and driving and advertisements warning people of the health hazards of smoking.

7) A company might have specific product marketing objectives, e.g., transforming negative issues into positive ones and thus increase sales.

8) Example: Overcoming the negative image of disposable plastic cups by making potential customers aware of their benefits - no washing up, ideal for children's parties, no worries about damaging the family' s glasses, excellent for picnics and available in a variety of colours.

Summary Of Marketing Objectives

The following is a range of marketing objectives which are dependent on the overall business objectives:-

1) Build brand recognition - theme or logo
2) Repeat purchases - the customer purchases the product regularly
3) Gain market leadership
4) Increase market share
5) Dominate the market

Marketing Decisions And The Link With Other Parts Of The Business

As any marketing decisions would affect the rest of the business, they would have to be considered in the light of other parts of the business.

Production

1) The products marketed by a company have to be manufactured by the production department according to the customer 's specifications or requirements.

2) If it could not do so or it were unable to manufacture the products in sufficient quantities to meet customers' demand, it has to subcontract the manufacturing to another company.

3) For example, Wispa was so popular when it was launched in the early 1980s that Cadbury withdrew the product for two years while gearing up its production to meet the great demand.

4) Certain products are expected to have an aesthetic design, besides being technically sound, e.g., houses.

Finance

1) Marketing requires extensive research and advertising which cost money
2) The finance department has to see to it that the various departments do not spend beyond their respective budgets.
3) Otherwise, it might have to raise more fund, which would in turn add to the cost of the product.

Personnel

1) As there is a need for the company to keep in close contact with its customers, an efficient, ambitious, competitive and aggressive sales-force,

able to generate bright, innovative ideas, is needed, and has to be recruited and continually trained.

Market Aggregation

1) Some companies would sell only one product to the whole market.

2) For example, Rowntree and Nestle, have been famous for a variety of branded sweets, for instance, the Polo mint, which had one type of packaging and one flavour.

3) Marketing such a product to a total, or aggregate, market is known as undifferentiated marketing.

4) After a drop in sales and the increase in popularity of a competitive product made by Trebor, Nestle introduced three new versions of the Polo mint and made a serious attempt to dif ferentiate the marketing process by targeting different customers with the wider range.

Market Segmentation

1) Market segmentation is the subdivision of a market into separate and distinct groups of customers who each have a distinct marketing mix.

2) Customers now have more choices.

3) Companies have to have more information about their customers in order to understand their needs and wants.

4) For example, a company marketing train journeys has to have the following information - age of travelers, traveling times and willingness to pay extra for more luxurious accommodation.

5) The train service company could, with this information, chage a range of prices to the different categories of travelers.

6) The following are examples of market segmentation:-

   a) Geographical Segmentation

      i) Geographical segmentation is targeting a particular region of the country for customers who display similar purchasing habits, e.g., the purchase of drinks.

      ii) Customers' preferences vary from region to region, e.g., drink preferences, preference for train travel and preference for car travel.

      iii) In market segmentation, the company sells a product to the people in a segment or certain segments of the market who have a preference for it.

   b) Demographic Segmentation

      i) A market could be divided according to the characteristics of the population, e.g., age, sex or income.

ii) For example, different types of soft drinks could be marketed to the different age groups.

iii) One way of categorising customers, e.g., categorising by their income, is by using socio-economic groups, based on the head of each household's income - groupings based on occupations.

iv) The other method of categorisation is "The Family Tree", wherein segmentation is based on the particular stage in the customer's life, e.g., bachelor, young married, full nest (the full nest family would spend a lar ge part of its income on children and their upbringing and education), empty nest (the empty nest would plan for retirement and take holidays for two) and retired.

c) Psychographic Segmentation

i) This segmentation is more complex and involves considering the lifestyle and expectations of an individual.

ii) Various "descriptors", e.g., trend-setter, thrifty consumer, fashion-conscious, environmentalist, Yuppie (young, urban, professional) and DINKY (Double Income No Kids Yet), are used for categorising the customers.

Consumer Profile

1) A business would sometimes tar get particular consumers in order to achieve a greater market share, consumers whose life-styles suggest they are more likely to purchase the products of the business.

2) Example: Targeting the sales of screwdrivers to those people who undertake DIY.

3) A consumer profile consists of the following:-

i) consumer characteristics, e.g., sex, age, income

ii) spending details, e.g., products purchased, quantities and frequency of use

59. ECONOMIC ACTIVITIES AND MARKET RESEARCH

What Is Market Research?

1) Market research is the collecting, processing and interpreting of information which aids the decision-making process for the marketing of goods and services.

2) The market is always changing, e.g., fashions change and the business constraints change.

3) Marketing research should be a continual process.

Why Is Market Research Important?

1) To avoid losing sales, a business should anticipate changes in consumer tastes.

2) About seven out of every ten products fail.

3) Market research might prevent product failure, saving the business large sums of money in the long run.

4) For example, VNU, a publisher of computer journals, spent a large sum of money researching the needs of computer magazine readers and launched Computeractive in 1998, which gained a circulation of 200,000 within the first year.

5) Market research had shown that technical jargon was putting off many potential readers.

6) Computeractive's main selling point was the simplistic language which could be understood by all possible readers and not just computer "whiz kids".

7) Tetley carried out extensive market research by getting households to record their reaction to a new round tea bag. They launched the round bag nationally when the response was positive.

8) Market research would see to it that a product which would satisfy the customer would be produced and promoted.

9) Market research sees to it that the needs of the customer are taken care of when a product is promoted, thus ensuring its success.

10) A product might fail if there is no market research, e.g., the Sinclair 5.

11) Market research should ensure that there would not be errors, e.g., having brand names or expressions which connote undesirable things, for instance, Pepsi Cola's "Come Alive" translating into "Come out of the grave" in Japanese and Renault's describing a model as "pear-shaped" translating into "twit" in Italian, etc..

12) Research could pin-point the cultural differences, such as the different ways tea is consumed in the U.S.A. (favour either iced or flavoured tea) and the U.K. (flavoured tea recently fashionable but not iced tea).

13) Market research is important in evaluating whether it is feasible to market a product.

14) It could help the business to gauge the reactions of both the potential and existing customers.

What Information Is Required?

1) Before launching a new product, the following information might be required:-

    i) Statistics on the size and growth or decline of the market.

ii) Existing company sales according to product, region or segment of market.

iii) How much competition there is.

iv) Existing and future product plans to ensure that new products fit with the company's product portfolio.

v) Government legislation and economic policy which might af fect the design of the product and the probable demand for the product.

vi) Etc..

Quantitative Research

1) This kind of research concentrates on getting data, e.g., number of customers, range of ages, what percentage of purchase, time of purchase, etc..

Qualitative Research

1) This kind of research involves getting information on reasons for purchasing a product, attitudes of customers toward a product, etc..

Further Information To Be Obtained

1) Market research could be utilised to obtain the following information (the "Ws"):-

i) Who would be the likely customers?

ii) What do they need?

iii) Why do they need such a product?

iv) When do they want to purchase the product?

v) Where do they want to purchase the product?

2) All this information could be obtained through desk research and field research.

Desk Research

1) Desk research is concerned with the collection, collation and interpretation of market data which have been published.

2) Such data are known as secondary data, as they have been collected by another business or body but could be used by dif ferent businesses for various reasons.

3) This kind of research concentrates on quantities.

4) This kind of research provides valuable background information and could be used to identify trends, e.g., the proportion of people using a product, the appropriate size of box to produce, etc..

5) There are numerous sources for desk research, e.g., the Employmen Gazette, the Central Office of Statistics, the Bank of England Quarterly Review, IMF reports, etc..

Benefits Of Desk Research

1) As such information has already been collected and compiled, it is relatively quick to obtain and therefore relatively inexpensive, though not all the information might be appropriate and some of them might be out-dated and thus not so reliable.

Field Research

1) Field research involves collecting primary data.

2) The collection of data by various techniques that are unique to the collector would be involved.

3) This type of market research is thus more reliable.

4) Data on the behaviour of consumers and their attitudes to selected products or services would be collected.

5) Field research provides essential information on the factors which affect the choice and tastes of consumers pertaining to selected products or services.

6) Through field research, a consumer profile which clearly indicates gender age, place of residence, income and expenditure patterns could be obtained.

7) With such information, the business could decide on the target customer for a particular product.

8) The business could thus segment the market.

9) Field research is sometimes referred to as the qualitative approach in collecting market information.

Methods Of Selection

1) Different methods of data or information collection are required, depending on the nature of the information to be collected.

2) Market research could involve testing consumers' reaction to a new product.

3) The research technique to be adopted depends on the attitude of consumers towards different products or their awareness of advertisements or products on the market.

4) The following are the main techniques which are used:-
   i) Questionnaires
   ii) Interviews
   iii) Observation
   iv) Sampling
   v) Consumer panels

Questionnaires

1) They could be used to obtain a wide range of information, from a

comprehensive profile of a consumer's lifestyle and expenditure patterns to a consumer's reaction to a meal which he has just eaten or a shop he has just visited.

2) The type of questions asked is as important as the way they are asked.

3) A closed question should be used if a simple answer is needed such as the gender of the consumer or whether he or she has ever purchased a particular brand.

4) A closed question restricts the way in which the answer is given.

5) For some closed questions, responses are given and have to be ticked.

6) This "tick box" approach is easy and quick to use.

7) It allows more consumers (respondents) to be asked in any given time period.

8) The tick boxes are also helpful when the data collected have to be analysed, saving time and money.

9) An open question could be used if a more detailed response is needed.

10) An open question is required when getting an explanation from a consumer (respondent), e.g., what about a product which appeals to him or why he purchased a particular product.

11) On the contrary, a closed question could obtain a like or dislike answer but not the reasons for the like or dislike.

12) Some questions might be biased due to their wording, e.g., "Why do you think a Range Rover is better than a Mitsubishi?"

13) Although using a questionnaire is a relatively efficient way of gathering a large amount of data, it is assumed that the person filling up the questionnaire or responding orally would have understood the questions and replied correctly.

14) However, the answers might not be correct or true, due to the lack of clarification (especially if it is a postal or "self reply" method), misinterpretation, and the inappropriate way the questions are phrased and the replies are solicited (which could influence the replies).

15) It is important to engage trained market research personnel or market research experts to design the questionnaire and carry out the collection of data.

Interviews

1) Interviews allow for clarification and an opportunity to ask supplementary questions which would ensure that a question is fully understood and the answer is thorough and helpful, especially when the consumer has become reluctant to purchase a particular product or he has changed his attitude towards a certain product.

2) The interviewer could read out the questions from the questionnaire and record the answers in an appropriate manner , ensuring that there are as little mistakes as possible (respondents filling up the questionnaire themselves are likely to make more errors).

3) If the set questions were asked in a certain order, the interview would be regarded as structured.

4) The interview is an unstructured interview when there is no set order for the questions or no set questions.

5) This kind of interview is informal and more relaxed, and could be more effective in gaining the opinions of the respondent.

6) The interviewer should be able to record information quickly, e.g., being able to write in shorthand, and accuratelyand be able to analyse the replies despite the lack of structure.

7) Though interviews are more time-consuming and therefore more expensive, the information collected is likely to be more accurate.

8) However, it might be difficult to get respondents who are willing to spend some time answering the many questions, and, it might take a long time to get a sufficient number of respondents.

9) There is the possibility that the respondents would rush their replies as the interviews progress.

10) The interviewers should be adept in ensuring that the attention of the respondents is maintained so that the required information could be elicited from them.

11) To avoid some of the problems mentioned above, as much interviews as possible should be conducted in the homes of the respondents.

Data Collection By Phone

1) Interviewing by phone is cost-efective - no travel expenses, more people could be questioned in a given time period and no inconvenience to the consumer (such as being interrupted during shopping).

2) But, there is the problem of intrusion in the respondent' s home, which not many people would like.

3) However, despite such a reservation, interviewing by phone has grown in popularity with market research companies.

Data Collection By Post

1) This method of collecting data offers the benefits of convenience to the respondent as the questionnaire could be answered at leisure within the comfort of the home.

2) Encouragement for people to fill up such questionnaires includes things such as free gifts, e.g., free lucky draw tickets, gift vouchers or free

subscriptions of Reader's Digest for those who fill up the form and return it within a given time period.

3) Most postal questionnaires include postage paid business reply service envelopes.

4) As the pressure on time is less, this type of questionnaire might well be rather long, and, it might be counterproductive if the questionnaire is too long, making it a daunting task to fill it up.

Consumer Panels

1) This kind of research is frequently used to evaluate the reaction of a consumer either to test a product which has yet to be launched and is one of a number on trial, or , to test a product which has yet to be launched nationwide.

2) The opinions of the consumers are normally collected over a period of time, e.g., Lever Brothers uses consumer panels to test a range of washing powders on a variety of consumers whose needs for washing powders vary.

3) For example, panel members are asked to test the washing powders and comment on the washing powders' ability to get the clothes really clean, produce the right amount of lather and whether its smell is pleasant.

4) The statements made by the panel members might take the following forms:-

i)   Inexpensive to use

ii)   Keeps colours bright

iii) Works well in low temperatures

iv)   Dissolves easily

v)   Rinses well

vi)   Removes stubborn stains

5) The replies would be sent back to Levers Brothers for analysis, in order that the needs of the different segments could be matched with the most appropriate powders.

6) To speed up the process of analysis, scaling is often used, which could take various forms, the most common being to attribute a mark to a given statement, usually out of 5 or 10.

7) On the other hand, scaling could be achieved by asking the respondent to tick a range of answers that are scaled during the analysis (and not on the questionnaire itself).

8) The scaling usually comes in gradations of approval or disapproval such as "agree" and "strongly agree".

Benefits Of Field Research

1) Field research provides specific information on consumer behaviour and attitudes.

2) This information should satisfy the specific needs of the business concerned.

Who To Ask?

1) It is important to get the appropriate information from the correct group or segment of consumers.

2) Each segment of a market would have specific characteristics and therefore unique needs.

3) Each market segment would require a distinct marketing approach using the marketing mix.

Samples

1) The market research's validity depends to a great extent on who are the respondents interviewed and how many respondents are interviewed, i.e., the quality and size of the interviewee or respondent sample.

2) The following are the sampling methods which could be adopted:-

Stratified Sampling

i) Select the group required, e.g., all males or all females, a particular age range or a particular area of the countryor even by postal codes.

ii) Then choose the actual people within the selected group at random (stratified random sample).

Random Sampling

i) Select the respondents at random.

ii) Since the respondents selected might not all be the type that the business wants to target, the validity of the random sample could be increased by having a large sample.

Cluster Sampling

i) A cluster sample is a form of random sample which is taken from a selected area.

ii) The selected area is usually considered to be representative of the population as a whole.

Quota Sampling

i) Quota sampling involves interviewing a particular number of people within a segment.

ii) For example, for age segment 13 - 15, select 50 males and 50 females, giving a total of 100, and, for age segment 16 - 18, select 50 males and 50 females, giving a total of 100.

iii) This is to ensure a more representative sample.

iv) This method of sampling is used when the characteristics of the market are known.

Convenience Sampling

i) Convenience sampling is getting a sample from the area which is the most accessible at the time.

ii) The reliability of this method is limited unless the information obtained from this sample of respondents is for a business located in the same area.

Who Collects The Data?

1) There is the problem of collecting information and ensuring that the information is up-to-date at the same time.

2) Collecting more information takes longer and thus costs more and the information collected could become obsolete during the time more information is being gathered.

3) Collecting less information would be quicker and cheaper and the information collected would not become out-dated so quickly though it might not be sufficient to ensure reliability.

4) This is the dilemma faced by the business which requires the information.

5) Up-to-date information is important for business decisions, e.g., decisions on having the products which customers want.

6) The business could gather this information itself or hire the services of a market research specialist.

7) It would depend much on the amount and the nature of the information required and the budget available for obtaining this information.

Sharing Information

1) As the cost of collecting information continues to rise, more companies now join together to share customer information.

2) For example, Jigsaw, formed in 1997, is a consortium for information on customer needs and includes Cadbury Schweppes, Unilever and Kimberly-Clark, who share their database information so as to build a direct contact with the appropriate customers, and, Let' s Play Together, which is a partnership between Proctor and Gamble (Pampers Playtimes) and Mattel (Fisher-Price) formed in early 1999, which not only share customer information but undertake a combined marketing campaign to launch Pampers Playtimes, a kind of nappy intended to allow the baby greater freedom of movement, which might mean that the child would be able to play more easily with its Fisher-Price toys.

Is Market Research Essential?

1) Some companies, e.g., Amstrad, refuse to carry out market research as they believe that consumers do not always know what they are answering and therefore their replies might be of little value.

2) Sony's Akio Morita ignored consumer research which indicated that there was no requirement for Walkmans, and went ahead and produced the Sony Walkman.

60. KEYNESIAN ECONOMICS

1) John Maynard Keynes was the "Einstein" of economics, a very important figure in 20th. century economics, an economist who had revolutionised the subject; he published his magnum opus, The General Theory of Employment, Interest and Money, in 1936.

2) According to Keynes, unemployment and slow growth in economic activity could persist over the short term and probably even for long periods and become ingrained in an economy.

3) This unemployment is also called demand deficient unemployment, as firms do not demand labour because consumers demand too few goods.

4) Keynes argued that reducing wages to deal with such an unemployment problem would not help as wage cuts would lead to lower incomes that in turn lead to lower planned expenditure, lowering aggregate demand and further lowering employment and raising unemployment.

5) He posited that since the economy would not be likely to correct itself if left to its own devices, governments should increase their expenditure, increasing aggregate demand, re-circulating more income so that the demand for unemployed labour would increase. (This is opposed to the classical economic view which advocated leaving the economy alone as it would right itself sooner or later.)

6) Keynes acknowledged the potential for problems of persistent budget deficits which might be generated by such a strategy.

7) As for the economy, Keynes argued that the economy could fall into an equilibrium in which output is low.

8) Each firm would like to produce and sell more goods at the current prices, but does not increase its production as it believes that any additional goods would end up unsold.

9) The firms thus produce few goods and employ relatively small numbers of workers.

10) The result would be that many workers are unemployed and aggregate incomes are low, making people unwilling to spend.

11) This would confirm the firm's belief that it is unable to sell more goods.

12) In this equilibrium, all producers are not prepared to hire more workers.

13) The new incomes which are generated by one firm's new hirings would have an insubstantial impact on the demand for its own goods, as well as an insubstantial impact on the demand for all of the other firms' goods.

14) The goods produced by the newly hired workers would end up being largely unsold.

15) On the other hand, if all firms were to hire workers at the same time, there would be a substantial increase in incomes and a substantial increase in the demands for all goods.

16) As for the rate of interest, Keynes believed that it is set exogenously by the central bank in accordance with certain economic indicators, such as the inflation rate (actual or expected), unemployment, or the value of the domestic currency, and not determined by productivity and thrift (the natural rate), nor by the supply and demand for money.

17) According to Keynes:-

    i) The rate of growth of autonomous demand determines the rate of growth of output.

    ii) The level of autonomous spending determines the level of output.

    iii) The autonomous components of investment expenditure, and government expenditure, determine the level of output.

61. FINANCIAL INSTITUTIONS (IN THE SINGAPORE CONTEXT)

Monetary-Policy-Making (Funds - Productive Investments)

1) MAS (Monetary Authority of Singapore)

2) Board of Commissioners of Currency

Operational Level

Wide variety of financial institutions:

(a) Commercial banks

(b) Finance companies

(c) Insurance companies

(d) Stock-broking firms

(e) Merchant banks

(f) Discount houses

(g) International Money-broking firms

(h) Leasing Companies

(i)   Factoring Companies

(j)   Gold dealers

(k)   Reinsurance companies

Actively participate in:

1)   Foreign exchange markets

2)   Asian dollar market

3)   Money and capital markets

4)   Securities market

5)   The newly established gold market

POSB and CPF - also active in financial markets

Basic role of financial institutions:

1)   Collect surplus funds.

2)   Channel them for investment in productive activities.

Finance companies provide:

1)   Loans for purchase of consumer durables such as refrigerators, TV sets, flats, houses, motor cars, thus stimulating related industries.

Financial Institutions

1)   Important components in economic structure of any nation.

2)   Provide system whereby funds can be ef ficiently channeled into productive investments.

3)   Provide mechanism through which nation' s monetary policies may be implemented.

Money Supply

1)   Money supply of economy depends on activities of credit creation and liquidity preference of financial institutions.

2)   Changes in reserve requirement imposed by monetary authority - strong impact on money supply by financial institutions.

3)   Appropriate adjustments of interest rates, the reserve requirements, and moral suasion.

MAS And Currency Board

1)   MAS, banker and financial agent to Singapore government, and banker to all the banks.

2)   Major responsibility - promote monetary stability conducive to economic growth.

3)   Supervises and regulates financial system.

4)   Administers all legislation related to banking and finance, including Banking Act, Finance Companies Act, Exchange Control Act, Development Loans Act, Local Treasury Bills Act, Insurance Act.

Board Of Currency

1) Responsible for issue of currency.
2) Issues and redeems currency notes and coins by virtue of Currency Act.
3) Under system, Singapore dollar is backed 100% by external assets.
4) Maintains Currency Fund to back currency-in-circulation and to meet redemption.

External assets in Fund:

a) Gold
b) Foreign exchange in demand and time deposits
c) Money at call
d) Treasury bills
e) Securities of foreign governments and institutions

Commercial Banks

1) Form largest group of financial institutions in Singapore.
2) Date back to 19th. century, not long after Singapore was founded.
3) Provide services essential to Singapore's development as centre for international trade.
4) Basic function: collect surplus funds in economy and current or time deposits, and extend credit to customers.
5) Facilitate payments by providing chequing facilities.
6) Offer credit facilities, e.g., overdrafts, loans, letters of credit, trust receipts, discounting of bills, and credit cards.
7) Others: Cash dispensers, safe deposit boxes, night safes, credit ratings, foreign exchanges, and investment management services.

Three categories of commercial banks:

a) Full License
b) Restricted License
c) Offshore License

Full License Banks

1) Authorised to transact whole range of banking business, including current, savings, and fixed deposit accounts, export and import financing, transfer of funds, foreign exchange transactions.
2) Locally incorporated banks and foreign banks which have been operating here for many years.

Restricted License Banks

1) Engage in most of activities of full license banks, except, not permitted to accept time deposits of less than $250,000.

2)   May not offer savings accounts, and are not allowed to open new branches in Singapore.

Offshore License Banks

1)   Offshore license introduced in 1973 - banks confined to foreign exchange transactions and doing business with other banks and institutions.

2)   Since 1978 - have been permitted to operate like restricted banks.

Finance Companies

1)   2nd. largest group of financial institutions in Singapore in terms of network of branches and total amount of assets.

2)   Became prominent in early 1960s - as a result of increase in demand for consumer credit.

3)   Most finance companies provide:-

   a)   Installment credit for purchase of motor vehicles and consumer durables.

   b)   Larger companies also provide mortgage loans for purchase of houses and flats.

   c)   More recently, some began to provide lease financing and account receivable financing.

4)   Obtain funds mainly by collecting fixed and savings deposits from public.

5)   Unlike commercial banks, not permitted to ofer current account facilities.

6)   Finance Companies Act - introduced in 1967 - to safeguard interest of depositors and to ensure that these institutions are under adequate control.

7)   Of 34 finance companies in Singapore, about half of them are subsidiary companies of commercial banks and the others are independent finance companies.

Merchant Banks

1)   Financial houses set up by wealthy merchants in England in 18th. century to provide funds for trading overseas.

2)   Over the years, they become involved in other activities and began to provide wide range of financial services, e.g., corporate finance, merger and acquisition, money market operations, investment management, international financing, corporate secretarial services, and gold bullion trading.

3)   In corporate finance, help commercial enterprises to raise loans of large amounts.

4)   Assist companies to seek listing on stock exchange.

5)   Advise companies on rules and regulations of listing.

6)   Act as underwriter of the issues.

7) In mergers and acquisitions - advise clients on conditions of such transactions.

8) Some also involved in money market operations, e.g., buying and selling of treasury bills, government bonds, and certificates of deposit.

9) Others manage provident funds and investment portfolios on behalf of individuals and institutions.

10) Also give advice on investment in stocks and shares, bonds and other securities.

11) Most have international connections and hence can arrange international financing for large-scale projects.

12) Also help foreign investors find suitable investment opportunities and partners for joint-ventures.

13) Many active in international bond markets, including Eurobond and Asian bond markets.

14) Some provide corporate secretarial services, such as share registration, nominee services and advice to clients on compliance with statutory regulations.

15) Existed in Europe in 18th. century. Introduced in Singapore in 1970 only, when Chartered Merchant Bank started operations.

16) Since then many formed.

17) By 1980, about 30.

18) Most are joint-ventures between local financial institutions and those from Britain, Japan, the U.S. and other countries.

19) Formed as result of encouragement from Singapore government whose policy in 1970s was to develop Singapore as an international financial centre.

Discount Houses

1) Discount market in Singapore - three discount houses started operations on 27 November 1972 with approval from MAS.

2) 4th. discount house in 1974.

3) Basic function of a discount house - to deal in short term funds.

4) Commercial banks and other financial institutions deposit funds with discount houses on overnight or callable basis.

5) Discount houses then invest these funds in short-term financial instruments such as treasury bills or other short-dated government securities, bills of exchange, and negotiable certificates of deposits (NCDs).

6) Prior to discount market, banks had to rely on direct re-discounting of treasury bills with the MAS when they were short of funds.

7) Can now buy from or sell to discount houses at better rate.

8) Operation of discount houses governed by two guidelines from MAS:-

    a) The gearing ratio - stipulates maximum amount a discount house may borrow in relation to its own shareholders' funds.

    b) The asset ratio - specifies proportion of types of assets that may be held by discount houses.

9) Discount houses play important role in money market in Singapore.

10) Provide MAS with smooth mechanism to regulate money supply.

11) With discount house operations, mechanism whereby net deficit or surplus among banking institutions at end of business day reflected in net position of discount houses.

12) A deficit is adjusted by MAS lending to discount houses.

13) A surplus is absorbed through selling of overnight treasury bills.

14) MAS also acts as a lender of last resort to discount houses.

15) Discount houses also enable banks to maximise their returns on short-term funds.

16) Also contribute to development of an active secondary market for short-term papers by facilitating issue and sale of treasury bills and government securities.

POSB

1) 1st. January 1877 opened.

2) One of oldest.

3) Encourage small income earners saving.

4) Means for them to invest savings and earn fair rate of interest.

5) Was then part of S traits Settlements Savings Group (Malacca, Penang and Singapore).

6) 1949 - Federated Malay S tates Savings Bank took over Malacca and Penang accounts, and with Unfederated Malay S tates formed Malayan POSB.

7) Singapore POSB - Separate entity , but still managed by Postmaster - General of Malaya.

8) After Singapore's independence - management transferred to Postmaster General of Singapore.

9) 1 January 1972 - POSB - statutory board - separate from Postal Services Department - managed by Board of Directors appointed by Minister of Finance.

10) Wide range of services - more than one million account holders.

11) Save-As-You-Earn Scheme (save fixed sum once a year) Annual interest and extra bonus.

12) GIRO - deductions for payments.

13) Lucky draws.

14) Safe deposit boxes.

15) Branches and service counters.

16) Computerised services.

17) Invest funds - government securities, bonds and equities in other financial institutions.

CPF

Types Of Financial Markets

The Money Market

1) Financial markets where lenders and borrowers of short-term funds are brought into contact with one another.

2) Deals in short-term funds and instruments (treasury bills, Singapore dollar NCDs, bills of exchange, and other short-term commercial papers and short-dated government securities).

3) Singapore money market comprises two major sections which are closely related:
   a) Inter-bank market
   b) Discount market.

4) Inter-bank market - Banks deal directly with each other or indirectly through money brokers.

5) Discount market - Banks, discount houses and the MAS.

6) At end of business day, commercial banks' excess funds are lent out to other banks overnight in inter -bank market, or deposited with discount houses on an overnight or on-call basis.

7) May also borrow from other banks and discount houses.

8) A commercial bank may need funds to maintain statutory cash balance required by MAS - thus, it borrows from other banks or sells some of its short-term instruments in discount market.

The Capital Market

1) Consists of two major sections:
   (a) Corporate securities market
   (b) Government securities market.

2) Corporate securities market comprises two segments:
   (a) primary, and,
   (b) secondary markets.

3) <u>Primary market</u> -
   - (i) Companies may raise funds by issuing shares to public or may borrow funds by floating corporate bonds.
   - (ii) Companies may also issue bonus shares or right issues.
   - (iii) Corporate securities market usually dominated by equities.
4) <u>Secondary market</u> -
   - (i) After floatation of a public share issue, company is then listed on Singapore Stock Exchange.
   - (ii) Public may buy or sell shares of listed companies on Sock Exchange and prices will be determined by supply and demand.
5) <u>Government securities market</u> -
   - (i) Government securities market - treasury bills, government-registered stocks, and government bonds.
   - (ii) Subscribers to these issues - banks, finance companies, the CPF , and other financial institutions.

<u>The Stock Exchange</u>

<u>The Asian Dollar Market (ADM)</u>

1) Financial market which deals mainly in U.S. dollar deposits outside the U.S..
2) Asian dollars dealt with in Asian financial centres.
3) Main centre for Asian dollars - Singapore, Tokyo and Hong Kong.
4) In Singapore, many financial institutions granted   Asian Currency Unit (ACU) licenses by MAS to deal in Asian dollar market.
5) ACU - basically an operational unit which forms part of the financial institution, but has to maintain separate accounting records for its transactions.
6) In Singapore, first ACU started in 1968 by Singapore branch of Bank of America.
7) Since 1968, many other foreign, as well as local commercial and merchant banks, have been granted such licenses by the MAS.
8) By end of 1980, already 115 ACUs in Singapore.
9) <u>Major objective of ACUs</u> - attract U.S. dollar deposits and lend them out for investment in this region.
10) Major participants in ADM - commercial banks, central banks, multinational corporations, international or ganisations or agencies, financial institutions and wealthy individuals.
11) Since 1968 - MAS actively encouraged the growth of market by granting <u>many tax incentives</u> to the ACU operators.
12) Phenomenal growth of ADM has greatly enhanced Singapore's status as international financial centre.

62. GENERAL USE STATISTICS (IN THE SINGAPORE CONTEXT)

1) Yearbook Of Statistics issued in July each year by Department of Statistics.

2) Contains figures gathered for past 10 years and covers statistical data on demographic, educational, economic, industrial and social aspects of Singapore.

3) Brief section on key social and economic indicators.

4) Another 16 sections on climatic conditions, population, labour force, national income, agricultural production, industrial production, utilities, consumption, construction and housing, external trade, transport and communications, finance and insurance, government expenditure prices, education, health and recreation.

Monthly Digest Of Statistics

1) Publishes most of data available in Yearbook.

2) 12 sections, ranging from demography to consumer prices.

Singapore Statistical Charts

1) Yearly publication by Department of Statistics - 1st. issued in 1978.

2) This book gathers in a concise and pictorial format some of important aspects of Singapore economy.

3) Its data taken from Yearbook and presented in form of histograms, pictograms, bar charts, pie charts, and moving average time-series.

4) Indispensable companion to Yearbook of Statistics.

Population And Vital Statistics

1) Provide most important socio-economic trends and characteristics of population.

2) Form backbone of planning and development of economic structure and social amenities.

3) Basis of all population statistics - census.

4) De facto census, i.e., census on actual number of people in country at certain date, including all those on board ships within the port limits.

5) E.g., 1980 Singapore Population Census -

   a) Conducted in May and June.

   b) Covered all persons living in Singapore on Census Day , 24 June 1980.

6) Information obtained includes geographical distribution of population, age structures, marital status, ethnic composition, housing pattern, employment profile, education standards, income level, religious affiliation, modes of transport to schools and places of work.

7) Census normally conducted at beginning of each decade.

8) In Singapore, 1st. census carried out in 1871.

9) 1980 Census was 11th..

10) Results of Census published in Report On   The Census Of Population, issued by Department of Statistics.

Vital Statistics - of births and deaths - include the following:

1) Report On The Registration Of Births And Deaths, And Marriages.

2) From the figures - estimate growth of population and thus enable policy-makers to plan for construction of schools, houses, and hospitals.

3) Report also gives population estimates by sex and ethnic groups at half-yearly intervals (end of June and end of December each year).

4) Report tabulates live birth statistics by sex, ethnic composition, mother's age, birth order, attendant at birth, and place of birth.

5) Also cross-classifications of live births by mother's age and birth order, mother's age and birth weight of child, father's occupation and birth order, racial group and place of birth, period of gestation and type of births, period of gestation and birth weight.

6) Report classifies death statistics by age, sex, ethnic group, marital status, occupation, and cause of death.

7) Civil and Muslim marriage records can also be found in Report.

8) Marriages shown by age, race, previous marital status, interethnic groups, and place.

Labour Statistics

Singapore Yearbook Of Labour Statistics

1) Contain labour market indicators and related statistics.

2) Covers areas of labour force, employment, unemployment, wages, industrial disputes, trade unions, factory accidents, and industrial diseases.

3) Labour force and economically active - all those 15 years of age and above.

4) Labour force classified by activity, status and sex.

5) Employment figures for both sexes recorded by age, industryoccupation, income, and qualification.

6) Cross-classifications of some of these characteristics, such as by industry and income.

7) Employed workers classified into three key industries:

    (a) Professional

    (b) Administrative

    (c) Managerial

(d)   Clerical, sales, services and related workers

(e)   Production, transport and manual workers.

8)   Average weekly hours and average earnings obtained by annual census of establishments.

9)   Unemployment data: age, race, qualifications -

(a)   Duration and type of job sought.

(b)   For unemployed working before, tabulation by previous occupation and previous industry.

10)   Job vacancies notified and filled.

11)   Membership of trade unions, with breakdown of size by union and by industry.

12)   Industrial stoppage statistics cover:

(a)   causes

(b)   durations

(c)   workers involved

(d)   man-days lost.

13)   Analysis of affected industries and of results of disputes.

14)   Factory accidents by industry, cause, and body site, followed by analysis of industrial diseases by name and industrial source.

Industrial Statistics

1)   Report On Census Of Industrial Production.

2)   Yearly published by Department of Statistics, first issued in 1959.

3)   Covers activities of industrial sector.

63. THE IMPORTANCE OF ECONOMIC THEORY IN BUSINESS

The Role Of Economic Theory In Business

1)   The interaction of demand and supply af fects all businesses, which to some extent are able to influence it.

2   Businesses have to observe carefully how consumers react to changes in th price of goods and gauge how price changes are likely to af fect the demand for their product or service.

3)   Understanding the market forces of demand and supply gives an idea of how the customer would behave, as well as the possible reaction of other businesses.

Demand

Changes In Price

1) As the price increases, the demand for a product might decrease.

2) If the price were reduced, the level of demand would increase.

3) Changes in the circumstances under which the product or service is bought could also affect the level of demand.

4) The actual or effective demand for a product is governed by the following two factors:-

   i) The ability to purchase (influenced by income or price).

   ii) The willingness or desire (influenced by choice).

5) A customer who has the desire to purchase a product but could not afford to do so cannot be included in the number of people demanding this product.

Changes In The Condition Of Demand

1) Besides price, other factors also affect demand.

2) These factors involve the willingness and ability to buy a product or service and are as follows:-

Income

1) The Demand For Holidays Abroad: An increase in the income of consumers would lead to an increase in the demand for holidays abroad.

2) If there were huge delays at airports due to a series of air traffic control strikes, there would be a decrease in the demand for holidays, as consumers would not want having to wait at airports for hours.

Advertising

1) The demand for a product, e.g., a soccer magazine, would depend on the individual's taste and choice.

2) Advertising a product could influence consumers to desire it.

Changes In The Season

1) The demand for certain products would vary according to the season.

2) For example, the demand for ice-cream could be expected to increase in the summer.

Changes In The Population

1) For certain products, e.g., products considered a necessity such as food, the demand for them would increase as the population increases.

Changes In Government Legislation

1) The sales of certain products, e.g., drugs or medication, might be regulated by the government.

2) For example, a manufacturer had to reduce the tablets in each box of medication sold, as required by the government regulation, resulting in

an increase in the demand for the boxes which hold the tablets, assuming that the overall demand for the tablets remained constant.

Changes In Economic Policy

1) Changes in the level of tax, e.g., for alcohol, cigarettes and cars, would result in a change in the level of demand for these products.

2) Government changes in monetary policy could make money harder to borrow, which would reduce the demand for products.

Changes In Attitudes And Information

1) The demand for products could be influenced by the reports issued by the various bodies, e.g., medical reports about the harmful ef fects of genetically modified foods af fected the sales of such goods almost overnight, leading to several of the main supermarket chains terminating their sales.

Changes In Taste And Fashion

1) Certain products, e.g., "fashion" goods such as clothes, come and go very quickly.

Changes In The Prices Of Other Products (Substitutes)

1) With many competitive brands or products available in the market, the demand for one brand or product could be greatly af fected by the price and advertising of another similar brand or product.

2) For example, if Crosse and Blackwell soups came down in price, the demand for Heinz soups could fall due to consumers switching over to the cheaper Crosse and Blackwell soups.

Complementary Goods

1) The price of one product could influence the demand for anotheras when two products are bought in conjunction with one another (complementary goods).

2) For example, CD players and CDs, fish and chips, pens and ink cartridges, and, cars and petrol are all complementary goods, i.e., they are used in conjunction with each other.

3) Example: A decrease in the price of mobile phones sold without a rental agreement results in an increase in the demand for phone cards which are necessary for making calls.

Derived Demand

1) Derived demand occurs when an increase in the demand for one product automatically leads to an increase in the demand for another product.

2) For example, an increase in the demand for houses automatically leads to an increase in the demand for land.

To consider the likely changes in demand, it has to be assumed that all the other variables which affect the product in question remain constant (ceteris paribus).

Supply

Changes In Price

1) Assuming that all the other factors remain constant (ceteris paribus), the supplier would be willing to supply more products at a higher price, as he could make more profit.

2) If the price falls, he might supply less products.

Changes In The Condition Of Supply

The following are factors which would cause a change in the quantity that is supplied regardless of the price of the product:-

Changes In The Productive Efficiency Of The Business (Improved Technology)

1) A manufacturer with new machines that could produce goods at a greater speed or a lower cost, or, improved production techniques (applying the concept of lean production) would be encouraged to supply more goods.

Changes In The Cost Of Production

1) Changes in the cost of production, e.g., changes in the cost of raw materials or labour, would alter the quantity of products the manufacturer is prepared to supply, assuming that all the other factors remain the same.

2) For example, a car manufacturer faced with an increase in the cost of steel would be less willing to supply cars, as rising costs mean less profit.

Government Legislation

1) If the government introduced a law requiring, e.g., all cyclists to wear cycle helmets, the manufacturers of cycle helmets would be more likely to supply more of these products.

Equilibrium

1) The market involves the interplay of both supply and demand.

2) Market forces should give rise to a situation wherein the demand and supply for a given product would be equal at a given price, i.e., at equilibrium.

3) The equilibrium quantity (q) is the number of products which:
   i) the supplier is willing to supply at the market price (p), and,
   ii) the consumers (demand) are willing to buy at the market price (p).

4 Businesses should be aware of the factors which might afect the price at which their products are sold.

5) The market conditions are constantly changing and thus require careful monitoring.

6) Businesses should pay close attention to the changes in the condition of demand and supply.

7) For example, if there were a promotional offer for The Times (which is a substitute for the DailyTelegraph), consumers would switch toThe Times and, as a result, the demand for the Daily Telegraph would fall.

8) It is important to note that the first thing to be af fected would be the demand for the DailyTelegraph (which has as yet no change in its price). The Daily Telegraph would encounter the following:-

   i) a new demand line to the left (D^1) - indicating a fall in demand (whereas a new demand line to the right would indicate an increase in demand),

   ii) a new *equilibrium point (Eq^1), and,

   iii) a new quantity supplied (q^1) - i.e., the quantity supplied has fallen (together with the above-mentioned fall in demand).

   (*equilibrium is the state whereby the quantity supplied is equal to the quantity demanded)

9) The change in the condition of demand has resulted in a decrease in the demand for the Daily Telegraph, and, as a consequence, its supply has fallen.

10) The final result is the price of the Daily Telegraph falling (to p^1) - the Daily Telegraph would reduce its price to prevent demand/sales from falling further. (To what extent the DailyTelegraph would change its price depends on a number of factors.)

11) If the manufacturer of a product, e.g., mug, is faced with an increase in the cost of raw material, this increased cost would affect the supply of the product in the first instance (a new supply line to the left, S, indicating a fall in supply).

12) The result of this increased raw material cost and the change (fall) in the supply of the product would result in an increase in the equilibrium price and, thus, a fall in the demand for the product (q^1). (To what extent the increased raw material cost would be passed on to the consumer depends on the product and the competition in the market.)

Disequilibrium

1) Disequilibrium is the situation wherein demand and supply are not equal at a given price.

2) For example, if the price of a product, e.g., potato, were increased (to p^1, suppliers would be encouraged to supply more of the product due to the attraction of more profit.

3) But, consumers might not be willing to pay this higher price.

4) The result would be a surplus or glut of the product (excess supply over demand).

5) If market forces were to push the price of the product down (to p^2), consumers would be willing to purchase more but the suppliers would be less willing to supply so many.

6) This would result in a shortage of the product (excess demand over supply).

7) The extra demand could encourage the suppliers to increase their prices.

8) In the end, the price would be increased to a point (p^e) where all the products which were supplied at that price (p^e) would be bought and, thus, the disequilibrium would be got rid of. (In other words, equilibrium is achieved after the price has been increased to that particular point (p - known as the equilibrium price) whereby the quantity supplied is equal to the quantity demanded - this quantity is called the equilibrium quantity

Market Failure

1) In the study of the interplay of demand and supply in the market, it is normally assumed that there are no interferences or external shocks in the market.

2) Market failure occurs when too many or too few products or services are available.

3) Market forces might result in some goods or services, e.g., medical care, beyond the affordability of many people.

4) This is considered a failure of the market as the product or service which is considered essential is not available to all who need it.

5) A product, or, service, such as medical care, e.g., is considered valuable and essential to the community at large and everyone in the community should be able to have access to it.

6) The government is one of the main "bodies" which both interferes with market forces and attempts to rectify market failures.

7) The government could impose a maximum price (reduced price) for the goods which it wants to make more affordable for more people.

8) To make sure that the supplier is willing to supply goods at this reduced price (e.g., a medical product which is "sold" at below the market price), the government provides a subsidy for each item sold.

9) The cost of implementing this artificial price is shouldered by the government and, ultimately, the taxpayer.

10) The wages of the workers in certain industries, which are normally determined by market forces, might be too low to ensure a reasonable standard of living.

11) Hence, the government might find it necessary to introduce the minimum wage for workers.

12) This is interference by the government in the market to "correct" a failure.

13) The minimum wage (p^2) would be above the market "price" for labour.

14) The government could rectify what are considered to be market failures in the distribution of income within the economy by operating a system of transfer payments. (T ransfer payments are money paid by the government in the form of benefits (social security) to the unemployed.)

ARTICLES TO STIMULATE
ECONOMIC REASONING

The world economy is now generally gloomy and depressed, especially some highly industrialised countries such as the U.S.A., Germany and Japan, while the more agricultural nations such as India, Indonesia and Malaysia are, relatively speaking, less affected.

The crux of the matter is that money held by people has to be spent or change hands in sufficiently large volumes for the economy to be buoyant. If people lose their jobs, have little or no money to spend and curtail or stop spending the economy would be in trouble. Equally bad is the situation where employment rate is high and people have money to spend but are hardly spending. The point is that governmental policies and aggressive advertising and marketing could only try to persuade people to spend more but the final choice of whether to spend or not still belongs to individuals. This means that our economic ills would continue to be intractable unless a more radical change in the monetary system is effected to ensure sufficient spending, besides the maintenance of full employment and/or the creation of more employment opportunities and other economic measures. Of course, to keep inflation at bay our supply of goods and services or production of output has to keep up with the expected increase in demand for goods and services as a result of this 'compulsory' spending.

Perhaps, two types of currencies should be introduced to ensure that there is sufficient spending. One type of currency would have an expiry date while the second type of currency would have no expiry date (as in the usual case). The issuance and administration of such currencies, especially the first type which has an expiry date, are to be the responsibility of a governmental monetary authority or statutory board. For example, the government could pass a law to the effect that all salaries have to paid in the following format: 70 per cent in currencies which expire say three months from the date of payment and the balance 30 per cent in currencies with no expiry date. The seller who receives the currency with expiry dates from the buyer could then exchange it at the governmental monetary authority for the following currencies: 70 per cent in currencies which expire in three months' time and 30 per cent in currencies with no expiry date. In this way everyone, bosses and employees, and, buyers and sellers alike, have to spend at least 70 per cent of their earnings within the allotted time frame of three months. Here we are only talking about salaries and purchases within the same country.

At the international level, where business between countries is concerned, the same principle should also apply, except that the currencies with expiry dates and the currencies without expiry dates should now be issued and administered by an international authority, for example, a newly created division of the United Nations.

This new monetary system should help to eradicate recessions, unemployment and other economic and related social problems.

(This article written by the author was published in a journal of the Royal Economic Society.)

In my earlier article I proposed a new monetary system for curing our economic ills. In this article, a further, complementary economic cure based on planned and concerted international economic cooperation is proposed. My country, Singapore, is still in the throes of an economic recession. Recession, unemployment, inflation, etc., are still the scourge of modern society here and have been so for ages. Can a more effective 'economic medicine' not be found that could permanently cure our economic malaise once and for all, instead of only offering a temporary cure with the expectation that the business cycle will return to taunt us in a few years?

It may be unfashionable but this is a plea that we, especially our governments, should manage the economy, instead of allowing the economy to manage us. At the macro level, we have to re-think and re-vamp our economic policies on a global scale, with nations consulting each other. The fact is that all the nations' economies are intertwined. All this signals a need for sweeping macro-economic revisions now if the status quo were to be eliminated. We should not take things lying down.

How about a world association to manage and co-ordinate the economies and economic activities of all the nations in the world, this association being represented by members from all the nations in the world? This association could fix or set quotas for imports and exports amongst all the world's nations. For example, the association could declare that Country A exports item X to Country B and Item Y to Country C and imports item S from Country B and item T from Country C, Country D exports item J to Countries E, F, G and H and imports item K from Country E, etc... with the quantities imported and exported amongst them stipulated, subject to periodic changes in the future.

I am not advocating replacing the price mechanism by the kind of state-imposed quotas and controls that produced the dire outcomes in much of the ex-communist bloc. What I have in mind is that all the governments throughout the world consult each other and work together with each other and meet each other's requirements by achieving the import and export targets set by the proposed world economic association.

In this way all countries in the world would have to produce sufficient goods and services to fulfill their own consumption needs as well as meet the quotas set by the association. Thus, there should be enough jobs and incomes for everyone, and, it would be a boost to the world economy and to world trade.

Finally, a rational economic system should consider the general welfare and economic well-being or safety of every human being in the world and should not have allowed some to wallow in vast wealth while some others are in abject poverty. The association I propose could also take into account questions of re-distribution and maybe provide a supplementary or even alternative aid mechanism. By encouraging a more even distribution of wealth, who knows, the association might even make a contribution to world peace.

(This article written by the author was published in a journal of the Royal Economic Society.)

3. DYNAMICS OF AN ECONOMIC DOWNTURN

We are now in the throes of an economic recession - the last economic downturn here had occurred ten years ago, whence, I now recall, there had been endemic retrenchment exercises by corporations. Keynes, the brilliant British economist, had held that the economy, if left to itself without government intervention, tended to end up with more problems, whilst his predecessors, the so-called Classical economists, had held the belief that the economy, if left alone, would always right itself or overcome all its problems; he had advocated governmental role in steering the economy smoothly, e.g., through expenditure on public works and fiscal measures. Keynes has been proven right now and again in having believed that the economy tends to go awry if left alone, as even with government intervention the economy still often goes wrong.

We know that it is not easy to get the economy going smoothly. Has not the U.S.A., e.g., been having world-class economists such as Samuelson, Klein and Friedman to offer it and the rest of the world excellent economic advice at the Council of Economic Advisers and why is it still languishing from budget deficit, unemployment and inflation (in fact, the U.S.A. is now experiencing the worst budget deficit in its history)? The influence of Lord Keynes' ideas had been paramount too in the U.S.A. during the late President Franklin Roosevelt's time, when the New Deal had been formulated with Keynes' guiding hand.

We may ask ourselves here, "Why is the economy all the time troubled by inflation, unemployment and the like?" We have made tremendous advances in science and technology, and yet we are no nearer to curing our economic ills.

Of late, there has been a great deal of publicity here in the press about workers losing their jobs through redundancy - the marine industry here has been the first to be hit by the world recession, having "hit rock-bottom" as far back as ` 82 - this year, ` 85, sees the going down of the electronics and building construction industries here. Some electronic manufacturing companies have reduced their working week (e.g., from five working-days to four working-days), some have retrenched, some have closed down or are planning to do so, the other industries are similarly affected. Many architectural firms and consultancies have also reduced their working week or retrenched staff, some have even resorted to reducing the pay of their staff to keep up with the hard time. Building contractors complain of shortage of contracts and contracts at "rock-bottom" prices. Developers adopt the "wait and see" attitude and are much more cautious in their investments. Even departmental stores and emporiums are not spared this painful fate - recently, the mammoth Emporium Holdings Group has carried out a small retrenchment exercise, and that, after the staff has pledged loyalty to the management at an elaborate company gathering. The situation is bleak. We now value our jobs and fear losing them; many of our friends, neighbours and fellow citizens are out of work or are in new jobs at lower salaries.

How does all this affect us? Of course, the unemployed are likely to feel frustrated and worried. The employed also seem worried about their future - who knows when the axe is going to fall? Everyone seems more cautious about spending. When money does not change hands fast enough in the economy, business would not be viable. Businessmen are also more hesitant in their ventures; staff who have resigned may not be likely to be replaced; spending on new equipment and/or expansion programs are also likely to be held back. All these people who are affected by the economy will in turn affect the economy.

At this point, Keynes, if he were living today, might have urged governments to spend more on public works, create more jobs, or reduce taxes, to increase purchasing power and consumer demand, to prop up the economy. Has not the U.S.A. been doing that for years, so much so that it is now facing the worst budget deficit in its history? Keynes' ideas do not seem to have worked well in the U.S.A.. Have they worked well elsewhere? Are they likely to work well at all, at least in some places? Our time is different from that of Keynes and may require a different set of solutions.

There seems to have been too much adverse publicity from all quarters, especially the press, and this does not seem to have helped our economy in any way. Government leaders and other opinion leaders may have been unconsciously "dooming" the very people they hope to bring salvation to by painting too many "dooms-day" pictures for them. This makes everyone neurotic and pessimistic. This kills business adventurism, business enterprise, as businessmen over-react in response to all this.

Several years ago, there had been a great deal of publicity here about the booming building industry - the press talked about it, everybody spoke about it. The result - many people set up building-supplies companies (I myself have been approached to help set up a scaffolding-manufacturing company) - many building construction foremen and managers gave up their secure jobs to set up their own building construction companies. A few years later - now - they are caught by the economic downturn that more or less took everybody by storm.

It is all psychological. If, e.g., there were rumours, even unfounded rumours, that a certain bank is financially tottering, would not every account-holder of that bank rush to withdraw their savings out of fear? This analogy is aptly applicable to the economy.

Publicity and opinions of an adverse nature should thus be carefully regulated to prevent or minimise repercussions in the economy. Prophets of doom, pessimists and, generally, people with loud mouths or rumour-mongers of a perverse kind, should not be allowed to influence our opinions and attitudes to the detriment of the economy, of the people in general. How susceptible people often are. Just a few remarks from President Ronald Regan, and speculators may become wildly excited and jump to conclusions; his views, his policies, carry much weight and have a great impact on business, especially business of a speculative nature such as the share market. Keynesian theories may work up to a certain degree, but I feel that they ought to be reinforced by a government-conducted program of publicity or propaganda to maintain, boost, or enhance business confidence or confidence in the economy. On the other hand, the mass media should be persuaded or restrained from painting too many bleak pictures of the economy, if the state of the economy is not to be worsened by declining public confidence.

Overstatement of the economic conditions can be greatly damaging. Calm and optimism should prevail, and the government should play its role well, if the business enterprise is not to be disintegrated.

(This article written by the author was published in a journal of the British Society of Commerce.)

4. SOLUTION TO THE PROBLEM OF WORLD RECESSION

We in the democratic countries (socialist countries with controlled economies seem unaffected) are now troubled by a deep recession, and are experiencing job losses, business slow-down/liquidation and other related ill effects.

Recessions come and go in cycles and are like a dreadful epidemic. I often wonder why we must always be helpless victims to them.

I don't know whether most people are even fully aware of the causes of recession. One major cause is certainly lack of demand for goods and services. Obviously, there would be a lack of demand when people (businessmen, workers, and, even governments) "tighten their belts" (become more thrifty) out of a sense of insecurity in such bad times (they are saving more for the "rainy" days)!

Keynesian theories, which, e.g., advocate that governments spend more in order to create jobs and stimulate the economy, are normally not potent enough medicine for our economic woes.

I would therefore like to suggest the following stronger measures :-

a) At the "micro" level, the government could pass a legislation to the effect that the business enterprises and employed individuals must spent a fixed percentage (any reasonable amount) of their earned incomes on any and whatever things they wish. Certainly, this way more demand is created, and the economy is further stimulated. This could take effect on an adhoc basis till the economy picks up.

b) Similarly, at the "macro" level, countries, perhaps with the auspices of the UN (since there is no world government), especially those in trade blocs, could arrange to voluntarily spend a fixed percentage of their GNP on each other's goods and services for a certain period of time.

Instead of just griping about the recession in resigned helplessness, surely some of these measures could be considered, though implementing them would probably require concentrated effort and great leadership skill.

Governments could play a more positive role, as in the controlled economies.

(This article written by the author was published in the New Internationalist.)

5. SHOULD JOB-HOPPING BE REGARDED AS A BANE TO THE INDUSTRIES?

Job-hopping is often ascribed to the irresponsible attitude of workers. How much truth is there in this?

Isn't job-hopping somewhat inevitable since our labour market is a free one, where the forces of supply and demand have free play?

Also, labour mobility is in some ways necessary to any economy, although it must be subject to reasonable restraint.

Entrepreneurs would not be keen on investing in a country or in expanding operations there if there was not a remote possibility of their attracting experienced workers from other corporations.

163

The companies which lose workers may complain but those who are hunting for workers may bask in the satisfaction of meeting their labour requirements.

Another point to bear in mind is that labour mobility helps to ensure a better spread of available talent in the country.

If favoured and important industries face serious labour shortages, the government may even encourage workers from other sectors to join such companies.

This may be called redeployment of labour but when workers move of their own accord, it is called job-hopping.

So, labour mobility is a relative thing that may be viewed differently as circumstances change.

On principle, employees should have freedom of choice just as employers have the right to hire and fire their employees.

While employees should adopt responsible work attitudes, employers should also play their part by adopting an enlightened approach to personnel management.

It is after all the employer who determines the conditions and pace of work. They can either motivate or de-motivate workers by correctly assessing skills and abilities and by reading intelligently the psychology of workers.

They should also be aware of poor human relations at the work-place which seems to be often overlooked.

Workers leave their jobs sometimes because they cannot get along with their colleagues or their bosses or both. Not everyone likes getting involved in office politics. Those who do not get into it, get out.

We should thus take a deep look at the causes of job-hopping before we begin to blame job-hoppers for their irresponsible attitude, as has often been the case.

But there are errant employers who contribute to job-hopping. Some employers may have bad attitudes too, and are not incapable of mismanagement.

To help resolve this problem of job-hopping the employers' federations and the unions could draw up codes of conduct or ethics for both employers and workers who should adhere closely to them.

After all, job-hopping is not always bad. Sometimes it is desirable, for the reasons given above.

(This article written by the author was published in a British management journal.)

6. FINANCING NEEDS OF SMALL INDUSTRIES: ARE THEY BEST SERVED BY A SPECIALISED INSTITUTION?

There must be division of labour. There must be specialisation. There must be international trade or exchange. There is the necessity for inter-dependence in global affairs, be it scientific, political, economical, social, and so on. Today, industrialisation has a greater and more important role to play than in days of yore whence agriculture was the mainstay of the world's economy. Since the Industrial Revolution, things were never quite the same again - the tip of the balance in economic affairs has since been weighed down with a different emphasis. Now, we are thinking in terms of a second industrial revolution, or, for some more advanced countries, a third, or even, fourth industrial revolution.

The cardinal point is that industries have to make a start somewhere in time - since the Industrial Revolution, sweat-shops and cottage industries have evolved into bigger manufactories or manufacturing organisations, many of which have grown through the ages into private empires, or, multi-national corporations, such as Du Pont and General Motors. This entails the broad vision, daring and entrepreneurial capability of a few talented people of sharp business acumen. Of course, not everyone can be a financial genius.

For those who have seen through the tough, worrisome days of financing and running a concern, no matter how insignificant in size, it must have been quite an experience. To have a sure grasp of the intricacies of the business you are in, to dump practically all your life's savings and, probably more than that, if loans are to be taken into account, into the business, to anticipate the possibilities of making it and the pitfalls, to predict, or try to predict, public reaction to what your company specialises in, certainly are no meagre task for otherwise, each and everyone of us would be our own bosses rather than earn our own meagre living by being employed by these so-called entrepreneurs. We may think ourselves expert in any one or so of the above-mentioned fields or aspects to a commercial activity. But it would be rather a difficult thing for us to be rightly so an authority on all these. Here again, there is the question of opportunity. Born into a business family, a person may be more likely to acquire these capabilities, if he has an aptitude for it - this is likely to be due to no small part from the encouragement from the family to get involved and help out and from the sheer sense of power that can be derived from running or helping to run a business. One tends to feel that if one can run a business, runs it well and acquires much wealth, one can do almost any other thing with similar ease. This may give a false sense of security. But, nevertheless, it nurtures a self-confidence which is a prerequisite for a would-be or budding entrepreneur. It is similar to the certitude a successful insurance salesman feels about his ability to sell other things, insurance sales being one of the hardest types of sales.

It would indeed be unwise to try to do too much too quickly, as far as entrepreneurship is concerned. I cannot, for instance, if I were to invest my capital, invest it to the extent that General Electric or Philips has done so even if I have a very vast coffer. I can only take a cautious step forward. And it may be many more years before I can really run. Alternatively, I may not be able to take this sure step forward at all; maybe, I can only crawl. I would need the technical know-how, the in-depth knowledge, I would have to learn about the market, the investment potential, I would have to consider how much risk I am prepared to take, I would have to have the capability and the means of securing loans through banks and other financial institutions. There is a myriad of other items to look into.

There is a tendency today to pay too much heed to the big, well-established corporations, many of whom are feared by governments because of their awesome power over the masses in providing jobs, training and social benefits - this puts them in a position to dictate terms to governments. It seems that people have forgotten or overlooked how they were once insignificant digits of business enterprise. Today's sweat-shop or small industry may very well be your mighty multi-national corporation of the future. But the stiffer competition, which is a direct result of the population explosion, in business, is not making it any easier to expand, or even to survive.

However, many things can be done to stimulate their growth, especially by the home government. For example, tax incentives can be given to small industries, to encourage their growth. Special training schools can be set up to train people for such industries. Interest-free loans can be made to them by the government. Quotas can even be imposed on certain imports so that these small industries are not wiped out by the much bigger competitors from abroad. Certain governments, it must be pointed out, simply believe in autarchy, and they have to put in an intense effort to see that their industries, be they big or small, thrive, though their wisdom in this respect may be doubtful; and hypothetically speaking, if by a strange twist of fate, the countries, which depend a great deal on international trade, should suddenly depend less so on international exchange, and suddenly turn to autarchy, there will result a situation whereby the world as a whole would enjoy less of the totality of goods which would only be enhanced by international trade. Though autarchy, it must be pointed out here, may make a nation less dependent on other countries, it is likely to be of less value to mankind as a whole as it is selfish and tends to create the conditions which cause international conflicts, and it also tends to impede progress for the human race as a whole because international co-operation would be lacking, under such a condition. But, in autarchies, there is a likelihood that small industries will play more important roles than would otherwise be the case; with the government's intention to make the country self-dependent, certainly, any industry, no matter how insignificant it may seem to be, would be relied upon to perform a social role in providing the necessities and goods for living; the small industries would not be likely to be taken for granted and would have a more positive role to play, and they would be an integral part of the closed economy.

Small industries vis-a-vis the bigger corporations today find difficulty competing with the latter. Obviously, difference in financial status makes all the difference. The small industries face very serious problems as a result. The big corporations have little or no problem getting loans from financial institutions because of their reputation whereas the banks would be generally more cautious about loans to the smaller companies. As the saying goes, "Money makes money". Hence, the more capital you have, the more money you can make. Expansion, for the big corporations, would hardly be a problem at all. But to the smaller companies, expansion has to be carried out with more care, due to their more limited resources.

Another factor is the difference in organisational structure. In the big corporations, a well-ordered, clearly-defined organisational structure can almost always be discerned, with many departments performing well-defined functions and very diverse functions too - hence, you may find a sports and recreation department, a public relations or community relations department, a workmen's compensation department, a safety department, or, even, as in big shipyards, a fire department. It is not surprising that some of these departments may even be bigger than a small company, in terms of sheer manpower. There is, in other words, bureaucracy, which is bad if it is over-done. Contrariwise, the staff and managers of smaller companies may be all-rounders, and over-worked all-rounders too, each performing wide and diverse functions. Because of this, there is no sense of orderliness, which turns the more ambitious employees off. This is probably because the smaller companies cannot afford to have too many departments, because they cannot afford to employ so many staff-workers. Big companies often have a reputation to live up to and preserve, hence, they have to maintain a good corporate image through their public relations department whereas a small company is a small company and over-staffing may force it to close down sooner.

Because of the vast resources available, many big corporations can afford to set up their own research and development departments. It is a case of advantages leading to more advantages. In the case of the big corporations, the advantages of wealth seem limitless. Lockheed can afford to bribe governments. General Electric can dictate terms to governments. Many can afford to employ scientists at lucrative remunerations to do nothing but think, think of better designs and better products, which can out-rival their competitors - a scientist may only produce one or two excellent ideas in two or three years and yet such corporations find it worthwhile to put him on their payroll. At the moment in Singapore, research and development do not seem to loom large at all in corporate life and seem practically non-existent in the small industries, which, of course, could hardly afford to employ people to do nothing but think, such a seemingly unproductive activity.

The big corporations, because they provide jobs for many hundreds and thousands of people, can certainly pull the strings. They have the muscles to manipulate the economy, especially if they are conglomerates with wide-ranging business interests, employing thousands. Many are, in fact, governments in their own right. They provide you not only income if you work for them, but products and services which determine your life-styles and fashions. If you are dowdy, Lee's can make you more elegant, at least it can make you so in the eyes of fashion-conscious people who may equate elegance with Levi shirts and pants.

But, what about the small corporations, the dwarfs amongst the industrial Goliaths? They are out-shone and over-shadowed by their gigantic brethen. They generally do not enjoy the esteem of the populace, so much so that people often prefer the more expensive services and products of the bigger companies simply because they are considered more trustworthy in terms of quality standard.

Much worse than all these, the small industries, especially in Singapore, seem in great danger of being extinct. Obviously, governments encounter greater pressure from big corporations and it would be much wiser to be with the big corporations than to be against them. Many governments of Third World countries learn and import technologies from the big multi-national corporations, many of which are leaders in technology in their own right. In the light of all these, what place in society do the small industries really stand? Probably, they are at the brink of industrial death, especially so in Singapore, where they are encouraged to expand, or else, they are coerced into phasing out, what with the acquiring of private properties, old shop-houses and dilapidated factory-sites for urban renewal by the government.

Perhaps, this government is not interested in the small industries. Or, they give up hope on them. Ironically, however, many of the big multi-national corporations still turn to these supposedly insignificant industrial organisations when they are faced with production "bottle-necks" - many small industries are actually the sub-contractors of the giant corporations. The role of the small industries seems very much under-rated. But if the small industries are suddenly extinct who would be relied upon to play a supportive role in industrial society? The small and mini industries have to be nurtured and encouraged to play more important roles. Surely, by doing so, the government can diffuse some of the awesome power of conglomerates. This is the only way, perhaps, of diminishing monopoly or oligopoly power. And this is a positive benefit to consumers and society who need not unduly pay through their noses for consumer and luxury items and who can expect better quality from their purchases. The multi-national corporations do not owe any government any living. They fear practically nobody. Worse still, they are held in awe by people and governments. Why allow them to be more powerful and more fearsome by letting the small industries die? After all, the latter can act as a counter-balance economic force. We need not have to reckon with the economic power of the multi-nationals. All that would be desirable is more healthy competition from the small industries. Only with such conditions, perhaps, will the necessary evils of capitalism be diminished.

In the United Kingdom, there are over six hundred banks which specialise in serving the industries. The banks tend to favour the industrial giants, which of course is natural as they have their profit motive in doing so. The public image of small industries does not appear distinctive and it is dubious that some of them have any image at all. At best, people can only envision a rather less than positive image of such corporations. Insufficient efficiency. Lack of organisation. Haziness. These are the abstractions that tend to swamp the public mind as regards the small industries. But the ironical fact is that there are some small industrial organisations that have performed remarkably, but how many really notice them? Such an image of the small industries seems irredeemable.

It is up to a specialised agency, most probably a government agency, to salvage the image of the small industries. This should be the initial measure towards positive growth. A good public image definitely is conducive to greater marketability of products and services. The root problem of small industries is of course finance. With greater resources, presumably, most of the problems would be solved. When institutions such as the World Bank and the Asian Development Bank can devote their activities towards promoting the economic welfare of the underdeveloped and the Third World countries, why can't a government bank, or a government central bank, like the Development Bank of Singapore, help to promote the growth of small industries by providing relatively cheap and readily available funds? A multi-farious agency of the sort that is a cross-breed of the National Productivity Board, the Economic Development Board and the Development Bank of Singapore would be ideal. There must be a conscientious drive towards nurturing the small industries, which are at the moment at the cross-roads between dying and surviving. These are all of course taken in general terms. It is idiocy to destroy the future of the small industries as it would inflict self-harm to the economy. The viability of small industries should be a desired end in itself, and as the consequences of their viability are of a national nature, the government has to formulate national policies that ensure their flourish. It is not to the national interest to nip such economic flowers in the buds. Doing otherwise would benefit everyone in every conceivable way. The small industries which are mostly local-owned should be given the opportunity to form the spine of the economy. If too much foreign investment is relied on, what would happen when foreign investment is re-channeled to other countries with cheaper labour and more relative advantages? Can we afford to run such great risks at the expense of the smaller local industries? These are disturbing questions enough; though at the moment the economic climate for foreign investment here is in peak condition, it does not mean that the government can afford to be so complacent that they treat the small industries as economic non-entities. It is essential to overhaul the public image of the small industries. The Economic Development Board has sold Singapore well to the international community; hence, the sea of foreign investments. Likewise, this proposed government agency that ought to be the saviour of the small industries should execute a blitz of public relations campaigns abroad to sell the small industries to the international community. To seek new and expand existing markets, so to speak. This must be a pre-condition for future growth.

By providing cheap and readily available loans to the small industries, it would make it easy for the small industries to conduct their own intensive public relations programs, which at the moment are practically non-existent. Once their public image is glossened, economic and financial growth is inherent. And with firm backing from a high-powered government agency as such, this is not likely to be a distant possibility.

After the paramount task of image-making, there are a host of other needs for the agency to look into. The need to train personnel for the small industries is not to be overlooked. Too often only the big corporations sponsor their staff for specialist training, to upgrade their skills. It is time that the small industries be given a helping hand to either sponsor their staff for special courses or conduct courses for their staff. A training centre can be set up for this purpose and the National Productivity Board is a good model to follow. It is the finely-honed skills of their staff that ultimately ensure the survival and expandability of the small industries.

Another aspect is technology. The big corporations are strong on computerisation. This is the age of automation, of labour-saving, cost-saving and time-saving technology. And with automation productivity is expected to improve manifold. Unfortunately, many of the small industries have stopped growing, technologically, since long back in time. The bigger industries can maximise their production with minimal costs, while the smaller organisations do not enjoy such marginal efficiency of capital. How are they to compete in the world market with outdated technology which results in high production and labour costs and second or third rate products? The conglomerates could afford to throw money on research and development and automatic and more efficient machinery. They could afford to engage the best brains to do research on better production methods and better product designs. If the small industries do not try to keep up with their bigger counterparts, they are heading for extinction.

On the other hand, if they try to keep up with the pace of technological advancement, where can they find the huge chunks of funds to do so? Unless the proposed government agency provides the funds and, if possible, the facilities for research, it would only be by dint of something close to a miracle that the smaller industries can cope with the competitiveness of the industrial giants.

Obviously, the proposed agency would be saddled with a vastly complex task. They have to have the capability of convincing the small industries of the necessity for modernisation. What happens if the small set-ups are not enthusiastic about all this? Many small industries are contented with remaining small. Why ask for trouble? Why take more risks? But, if the small industries choose to remain complacent, instead of trying to modernise and improve, they may not be able to remain complacent for long; for they need not have to be complacent when they are closing down. Full government backing would be necessary. The agency, together with the government, must be single-minded in seeing the survival of the small firms. At the same time, they cannot over-play the importance of the small firms, such that foreign investors feel antagonised. Small and big companies each have their separate roles to play. There have to be nuance and subtlety in the words and deeds of the proposed agency.

It would probably be better still, if the agency has the additional mentorship of a world institution such as the United Nations or the World Bank. For it seems essential that the concept of the usefulness of the small industry and its social significance find acceptance at every level and location of human society. There should be a superfluity of activities aimed at promoting this concept and what better organisation or organisations than the above-mentioned to carry out this important public relations task.

It is hardly beyond doubt that left to themselves small industries would find survival in the dog-eat-dog economic world child's play. I am certain that small industries are socially desirable as they provide jobs, as well as goods and services, and if they are enlarged, more jobs and more goods and services could be provided. The ultimatum of modernisation and progress for the small industries would be more of the good things in life for everybody.

To tackle these challenging tasks, the proposed agency should combine the efficiency of a banker, a trainer, a public relations manager and a marketing manager. This specialised institution may yet bring a new era in economic affairs or a new economic order.

7. THE KEYNESIAN THEORY

John Maynard Keynes was a brilliant economist of the thirties. His ideas revolutionised economics. He brought an about-turn in the conception of politicians and economists regarding the economy. Starting from Jean Baptiste Say, brilliant French economist, the concept of economists thenceforth was that the economy tends towards full employment and equilibrium in market conditions. Keynes was to theoretise and prove that this was not the case. His many predictions about the British economy turned out to be true. Ironically, his theories were being practised by Hitler, consciously or unconsciously, and the result was just what Keynes predicted - full employment and high productivity in Nazi Germany. Perhaps, it was not a fair comparison, for Hitler was mesmeric and was able to rouse the people to heights of frenzy and was in effect a great motivator of man.

Unconscious to many, economics is the brother of politics, that is why it has been called "political economy". It is actually quite simple if politicians have that much power over the masses as Hitler had, in applying Keynes' theories. Keynes' theories would have brought thorough success everywhere.

But his ideas were good only for his time and not for all times, and modifications here and there are necessary. I would say that in order for Keynes' ideas to work, its advocate has to have the trust of and influence on the people. What is the use of providing ample employment so that full employment can be achieved when your people rather live on the dole than work? What is the point of pressing for higher productivity, when trade unions can dictate terms and twist arms, and workers are more interested in strikes than work?

A lot depends on the political skills of a country's leaders if all the factors of production, especially the variable factor of labour, are to be efficiently and effectively mobilised. People have to be moved towards achieving the ultimate desired goals by their leaders.

Contrariwise, if the people oppose the government more than they are being politically moved, much would be lost.

8. ECONOMICS SHOULD CHANGE WITH THE TIMES

The times of Adam Smith, Thomas Malthus, David Ricardo and Karl Marx saw the landlord class and the peasant-working class in opposition (class struggle).

Then the early nineties saw the problems of unemployment and depression.

Now, the culprit is inflation, which worsens chronically into stagflation, whereby inflation and vast unemployment create disaster in the economy.

This is evolution of political economy in a nutshell. What must economics deal with in the very first place, if it claims to be a science that is capable of solving problems? Jeremy Bentham and his disciple John Stuart Mill thought that economics must be concerned with the "greatest happiness for the greatest number of people". I am sure everyone must agree with them that economics must be concerned with this principle.

But this is quite often not the case. Capitalism may benefit only the few very rich people at the expense of the poorer ones, who are but "slaves" to their wealth-owning masters. Even governments have to respond to their beck and call at times because of the power over the economy they possess. When business flourishes, they recruit workers from all corners of the world if they could, if they are not available at home. When there is a recession, they will try to throw as much out as possible, jeopardising the livelihoods of wholly dependent families of the unemployed. Their control over the lives of their employees, they can make or break them, is almost absolute. They do not have to threaten you or manhandle you. But they can starve you by simply plucking you out of their payrolls.

It is strange that a long line of economists from Adam Smith to John Maynard Keynes, to Milton Friedman and Paul Samuelson, who have worked hard at solving the problems of economic survival, have hardly solved the world's economic problems. It appears like a case of a problem solved and a new problem cropping up. In the last analysis, it is the people who create their own problems and people are so unpredictable. The U.S. has redoubtable economists like Samuelson and Friedman and yet its economy has been tottering. Where is the importance of fine economists and their theories? Economists may act as policy advisers to governments and rulers but governments and ministers need not act on their advice and would only promise and carry out what is politically expedient.

The society at large is getting more and more complex, of course, and with it too goes the economic problems. Capitalists and entrepreneurs are now faced with very demanding consumers. Now consumers try to go for excellence in styles of living. They simply refuse to watch black and white televisions and must enjoy the psychedelic delights of colour on televisions. Cars must come in style and modern designs. Clothes must be stylish and fit well. They want to buy things that are cheap but good in quality. They are very much more selective in consumption. They force factories and companies to close down by simply not buying their produce, which in turn leads to vast unemployment and great social problems. This in turn would adversely affect the consumers who are responsible for forcing the companies to close down. The cycle is a vicious one.

There is so much in the world to be done. Yet, so much talent, so much energy, is not made use of, and so many people have to go unemployed! If only corporations and government provide meaningful employment to these people, employment that brings satisfaction to not only the employee but to members of society. For example, unemployed people could be employed to do social work by the government, such as caring for and looking after the aged or the sick. Yet, their services are wasted and they are allowed to idle around and to turn delinquent even. Often when such people offer their services and their skills, their potential employers turn them down. Human beings seem to be such that if they cannot build they have to destroy; they cannot be expected to sit still and watch things go by.

Basically, capitalism hinges around the profit motive. Bosses employ workers who are expected to make a profit for them, otherwise they are of no bloody use. Bosses are often so demanding on their workers that they resort to exploitation. You may ask, "Where is the ethics of everything that your employer generally does?" Employers may argue that if they do not demand so much of their workers, their workers would perform at their minimal and their companies surely could not survive then. Little do they realise that the more they press their workers the more their workers are going to resist them. If their workers are courageous and active, they could organise industrial action such as go-slow or strike, and if they are the more passive type, they would simply not put in their best. But, on the other hand, if workers are made to feel that they belong to the company, they would automatically put in their best and be proud and happy of doing so. But workers have seldom been given such respect and good treatment and inevitably productivity is always a problem with many companies whose managers have never learnt to treat human beings as human beings. The profit motive is thus evil when it makes so many human beings, the workers, unhappy, and this unhappiness would inevitably spill over to members of the workers' families.

The whole concept of entrepreneurship and capitalism is egocentric, and, hence social problems are always inherent when there is egocentricity. Entrepreneurs claim to be desirous of bettering the lot of society through their services or products, whatever they are, quite often. But if you examine their deepest motive, you are likely to detect the self-centred aim of achieving wealth and power for the self. In all fairness to entrepreneurs, who could be regarded as the key people in a buoyant economy, it would be appropriate here to mention that the profit motive is definitely a spur for them to take the risk of business enterprise, but certainly they could be educated to adopt a more humane and caring attitude towards the society whom they are supposed to serve. The marketing concept whereby the consumer is regarded as "king" must be the uppermost in their mind and heart, upon whose patronisation they depend for survival. But often when a wealthy person is firmly established in his business, his head is high in the air, and the consumer becomes "nothing" and he could "take it or leave it".

In the past, the serfs were the working-class, and the lords and nobles were the employers. Today, we have supposedly become more civilised and humane, we have supposedly ridded ourselves of feudalism, which is by all account oppressive, little realising that in our new economic order, a neo-feudalism has already arisen. Only because people who influence our lives greatly benefit from this neo-feudalism, they "pretend" to us of the non-existence of or pretend to be ignorant of the existence of this neo-feudalism. Employers through their powers of dismissal of workers could be just as oppressive as feudal tyrants, but today educated people seem to take such things for granted. Only the trade unions take some stand over this question of employers' authority and rights. And in some countries, even the trade unions are suppressed. How does the working class protect themselves against being oppressed then? Sociologists may argue for the benefit of hierarchy in society but this hierarchy tends to be problem-ridden due to lack of trust and suspicion between the worker and his employer. In actuality, many employers of workers believe or feel that workers would not put in their best if not pushed or instilled with fear. This principle, I sincerely believe, is wrong. For basically, humanity treasures the feeling of freedom and the ability to use their initiative. The wars for independence, revolutions and what-not, were fought for the sake of this precious freedom from oppression. Surely, these fighters did not expect new shackles on their descendants, surely, the oppression the wealthy and the powerful exercise over their underlings is but a reverting to the oppressionism of the feudal past.

Economics, in all common sense, should be concerned with the "greatest happiness for the greatest number", but in practice it is actually the "greatest happiness for the smallest number", at least, the economy tends towards the latter. For example, a business competitor to obtain maximum profit for himself would tend to preclude other competitors by such means as price undercutting and so on; similarly employees in competing amongst themselves for jobs tend to bring down wage rates. They say in business jargon that the big fishes swallow the smaller fishes. Trade barriers, closed-shop policies, and the like, aim to bring less happiness and hope to certain people so that they give up their attempts in their business and advancement endeavours.

In today's economic order, where competition is very keen, the survival of a company, an organisation, or even, a whole nation, depends on productivity, a very vague term, albeit a somewhat technical one. Economists speak of supply-side economics, in the United States of America, for example. Here in Singapore, the government and everybody in business emphasise productivity. What exactly is productivity? It could mean many things to many people. Nevertheless productivity is the key to today's economic survival. Even if John Maynard Keynes, Adam Smith, Thomas Malthus, and the like, were living today, they would, in all likelihood, be recommending productivity. Productivity, for example, could be buying the cheapest raw materials and employing the cheapest labour. It could also mean the high motivation of the work-force which results in higher output. It could mean minimal input and maximum output. It could be incurring the lowest possible cost of production. It could be the greatest possible profit for the employer through tactical pricing. It could mean the introduction of better methods of production or automation. It could be the reduction of labour. It could be re-organisation. But in simple, basic terms, it means the best possible profit for the entrepreneur, i.e., it is up to the entrepreneur to decide whether he should maximise his profits at the expense of his workers, i.e., he resorts to exploitation, an unpleasant term to workers, or he should seek other means of maximising his profits without antagonising the workers. But more often than not, the workers would have to suffer because their employers want more profits or wish to retain their profits.

In actual fact, all workers would want to be treated fairly and be given the respect due a human, rational being. Employers, if they are really sincere, could persuade workers to accept pay-cuts in bad times, and accept fair increases in pay when times are better, as had occurred in some countries. But many employers choose to force their authority and policies down the workers' throats, being the almighty and unfeeling people they generally appear to be. As a result, much companies and organisations are suffering from industrial strife; at best, there is at least some strain in relationship or feeling of suspicion between workers and management.

The economic order of today should thus be concerned with good industrial relations and company welfarism. It is reasonable to assume here that good industrial relations and company welfarism would help to ensure productivity. It seems often the case that when a company does not do well, management blames its workers. But little do these people realise that how they manage the company plays an important part in the survival of the company; it is so convenient of them to think that they are capable managers and blame it on their workers when things are not turning out well, as has happened so often. When the general manager of a company resigns, the company could still function smoothly, but when only half the production work-force walk out, everything would be chaotic. Yet, management often regards itself as the key to high productivity and conveniently blames the worker when things do not turn out right. Should not management take the blame first before those under them are blamed? No. This hardly happens. Economists and governments should try to right this wrong approach if economics were to prove a really productive science.

Public relations and marketing would play very important roles in the economy, where business units are out to outdo each other and cut each other's throats. Even when there is no demand for a company's products or services, public relations and marketing must create awareness of these products or services in the people's minds, and ultimately the demand or greater demand for them. Marketing and public relations must be able to convince people that their products or services are better in terms of the quality, price, design, durability, etc., to create a demand or greater demand for their products or services. Many companies enrol their executives for management and marketing courses for their self-development, so that they could be more effective managers and marketers. Besides productivity and cost-saving, no company could afford to overlook the marketing aspect in today's tough business world.

But sometimes, advertising, public relations, and marketing could be carried too far and a demand for an undesirable or harmful product or service is created, which society would do better to be without. For example, the creation of too great a demand for cigarettes and liquor, both of which could bring serious health and social problems, could happen. In Singapore, because cigarettes cause cancer and other health problems, all cigarette advertisements have been banned, and cigarette manufacturers here keep a very low profile.

The classical economics of Smith, Ricardo, Mill, and the like, have been replaced by Keynesian economics, which are already being replaced by supply-side economics, which would yet be replaced in all likelihood by another brand of economics in years to come. The evolution of the science of economics goes hand in hand with the evolution of a society. Economics purports to analyse and propose solutions to the material problems of a society and intertwines with political theories and practices and social policies. Economics is concerned with the very basic needs of society, the acquisition of wealth which effects the acquisition of food, shelter, clothes and security. It is fair to say that without economic survival no other things could be made possible. No scientific advancement is possible when there is insufficient acquisition of funds for scientific research. You cannot produce good writers, scientists, astronomers, citizens, when your country is striven with vast unemployment and poverty. When there is economic chaos, you could expect crime rates to accelerate and political upheaval. That is why Keynesian theory emphasises government intervention in economic affairs, for it is ultimately the government that would be blamed and overthrown in a democratic election or, even, a coup d'etat, when it fails to solve its economic problems. Economic chaos foreshadows many other chaos in society.

It is sometimes hard to understand why there is so much unemployment in the world. There are so much problems to be solved and so much things to be done. Demand for new services or products could be created through public relations and marketing, which could mean job creation. If, hypothetically speaking, all the unemployed were employed to do social work, which is by all accounts meaningful and highly respectable work, how much social problems, not to mention the unemployment problem itself, would be solved; the unemployed could be employed, for example, in creches where they could look after the children of the employed, or they could be employed to look after the aged, the sick, the orphaned, the handicapped, the delinquent, and even the criminal, and how important and how appreciated their role would then be. It is hard to understand that while there are so much things that need to be done useful human resources are neglected by society and government. Economics should concern itself more with the social problems of the unemployed and the problems of society in general. The unemployed on their part must take up the challenge when offered such important tasks, and society must honour them for doing so.

Economic science is therefore of paramount importance. And no educated person should be allowed to be ignorant of economic reasoning. For in the last analysis, economic science helps to ensure the well-being, the survival, of the society at large. The new economics should always be concerned with new problems and, better still, it should prevent or avert new problems.

9. THE EFFECT OF TECHNOLOGY ON THE ECONOMY

Technology is changing so fast today that what is considered new technology would be out-dated within months. What does this imply? The individual has to invest plenty of time (and, possibly, money, if he were to attend courses and seminars on the latest technologies) in learning the new technologies - he undergoes what is known as "continual education" or "life-long learning". Time away from work, which would normally be his leisure time, is devoted to this undertaking, which not only means less time for relaxation and rest, but less time for his family and friends. Is this keeping up with the technologies to be regarded as a mental challenge? I beg to disagree on this point. The mind (and body) needs rest and release from tension. Such "enforced learning" which is to be continual could build up tension, even fear of being left behind by technology, and saps up energy. It is not going to be good for our well-being in the long run; though its mental challenge could be keenly felt in the short run, the stresses and strains of keeping up could negate this "uplifting effect" in the long run, what with pressure from family members and friends who demand their attention and time, plus the nagging fear of slipping behind and not being able to keep "up-to-date on the latest". Not being able to keep up with technology might mean becoming redundant and unemployed.

From the business or company point of view, keeping up with the technologies should mean greater efficiency and being one-up over business rivals. But this inevitably entails much investment in time and money - money to purchase new equipment that is the hallmark of the latest technologies, time and money to train staff on how to utilise the new equipment and how to make use of the latest technologies. Since there is a "learning curve" when new equipment and technologies are introduced, there would be a period, perhaps a short one, of inefficiency, when the staff has to grapple with the intricacies of the new devices. What is going to be disheartening is that after the staff has mastered the new technology in the next few months, the equipment or technology is beginning to become outdated, when newer, improved version(s)/model(s) of it are being introduced.

This is especially the case for computer software, which tends to be outdated within six months or so.

So, for both individuals and business organisations, the continual changes in technology means continual investment in time and money and extra effort in keeping "up-to-date with the latest". Technological changes have of course created new demands, e.g., demand for technological books, courses and seminars and demand for sophisticated systems or equipment and an high-tech, electronically enhanced life-style. Storage, retrieval and communication of information by electronic means are all carried out at unprecedented speed and scale. Are all the initial bogging down, slowness and inefficiency in embracing a new technology worth all the speed, efficiency and largeness of scale this new technology would subsequently bring? Do not forget that this new technology would be rendered relatively inefficient by the onset of a newer, better technology in the not too distant future. Generally, new technologies result in retraining of some of the staff while the rest are retrenched. A new technology generally not only boasts of speed and efficiency, but of lower manpower requirement (and, hence, lower labour costs). But do all these savings in labour, speed and efficiency outweigh the costs of investing in the new technology - investments in new equipment and training - investments which have to be continual in order to be able to keep up with the continual changes in technology? There is always a sense of uncertainty, tension, not knowing for certain where changing technology would lead everyone. Job loss and unemployment often follow the new technology.

Of course, life-styles have changed. Due to electronic networking facilities, it is possible to work from the home instead of reporting to the office to work everyday. At the push of buttons, we could turn on or off our TV sets, our doors and gates and many other devices. By the mere push of some buttons, we are able to manipulate objects, e.g., satellites, that are far out in outer space. And, many more.

It has been claimed that technology makes life easier for everyone. Is it really so? Could this be so when workers have to become grinds in order to be "up-to-date", instead of spending the time relaxing and resting, or spending more time with their families and socialising or spending their off-work time in voluntary work such as helping the underprivileged and the handicapped? Technology has changed our values. To remain employable, everyone has to learn new skills; in effect, everyone has become more self-centred - to compete well in the job market (or risk losing one's job), one has little choice but to acquire new skills and knowledge. Likewise, for the entrepreneur or the businessman to survive now, he has little choice but to acquire new technologies and engage suitably skilled staff. When would the chase for the "perfect technology" ever end? Would technology ever stop changing one day? Already many have lost their jobs because they did not or could not pick up the new skills for coping with a changed workplace. Many also have become unemployable because they did not or could not learn new skills, e.g., how to use a computer. For many, there is a fear of change, an inability to adapt to change, and a fear of or dislike for learning. Especially, the more elderly, whose habits and mindset have become fixed. This group, which might be large, is bound to suffer in this new technological age. The younger ones, especially those who just graduate from the technical institutions with the latest technical knowledge, are likely to be the ones who could adapt most easily to the current state of the technology, and they would have to keep upgrading their knowledge and skills in order to be able to ride the crests of the technological wave.

Many simple manual jobs have been taken over by machines, the result of the technological change. Before this, those with little or no education could earn a living by performing manual jobs. But even these jobs are getting scarcer and these manual workers, to survive, have to upgrade their skills to those of manning the machines that have taken over their jobs, which often require them to have some rudimental knowledge of reading and writing - they thus have to know how to perform simple reading and writing chores at least - or, they would be unemployed or unemployable.

The result of technological advancement is that sectors of the workforce have either been displaced by machines or by people who have the required skill and "leisure-time" has to be devoted to "life-long learning", which might not be fun. (What happens if one could not learn fast enough?) The job market is apparently more competitive - the number of available jobs cut down by automation or improved technology, the population growing exponentially, the technology changing faster than the rate at which it is mastered. On the surface, it appears that businesses, employers, benefit from the advanced technologies. But, even they apparently have problems keeping up, especially those with limited resources. They might save money on labour and efficiency, but all these savings might be eaten up by the further investments in technological upgrading.

On the surface, new, better technologies seem to portend a brighter, better, more exciting future. Probably, the advantage of new technology is only a myth. It seems to be something that is out of control, beyond the control of human society in general. It embroils everyone in a rat-race - race or be left behind. They say that science has never solved any problems - it only shifts the points of the problems elsewhere. This is never more evident now. Today, no one could rest on one's laurels and remain contented with what one has. One has to keep running, keep improving, to survive in the competitive world. There is much restlessness, uncertainty and insecurity. Life has lost its simplicity and has become much more complex. Is this really what we want? Or, have we been unwittingly led to this situation by circumstances beyond our control?

What would happen one day when technology evolves to the stage where it is beyond the grasp and control of the average human being, except for a minority? The ones who have invented these much complex technologies and the very few who have grasped and mastered them would have considerable powers and influence over the rest. They could be "dictators" in their own right. They might even be able to play God. Indeed, with cloning, man has already played God. This is not surprising, if you consider the fact that in any technological enterprise, the techie or technical expert is always well regarded by the big bosses - some might even have more powers than their big bosses, when they have become indispensable to their organisation - when their technical expertise and skills are well above those of all their peers.

Political power would remain in the nations with the technological clout, the leaders of technology. Even private individuals with technological clout, individuals with access to technological power, could wield considerable political power and influence. For example, Bill Gates, with his software empire, has changed the way we live and the way we are going to fight our wars.

So, is technological advancement a boon or bane to society? Doubtlessly, there have been benefits, such as better health and longer life-spans. We should not just look at these pluses, we should also look at the minuses, such as greater anxieties faced by those living in today's fast-paced world. On the whole, technology is not to be blamed. Man, who uses the technology, is the culprit.

Man must learn how to use technology intelligently and wisely, to minimise its ill-effects and maximise its advantages, rather than let it develop rampantly and run out of control. The key is to use technology to co-operate rather than to compete. But, the reverse seems to be true. Unless technology could be intelligently and wisely harnessed for the benefit of the whole of mankind, rather than just the selected ones who have the means to obtain or purchase it, leaving the rest without it to lose out or suffer in some way, technology would be more a bane than a boon to everyone. It seems that we are now more controlled by technology than in control of technology. This does not augur well for us.

Though the world economy is being fueled by technology, technology should be used wisely and with great circumspect, e.g., instead of causing fearsome job loss it should result in business expansion and job creation, the possible result of higher productivity and profitability. However, it now appears that having better technologies generally results only in being able to just compete and survive, i.e., companies have to strive harder to attain the same profitability, same result. Perhaps, the government could step in with incentives and/or subsidies to encourage such technologically advancing companies to expand and/or diversify, so that the excess labour resulting from technological change such as automation could be channeled to the new business expansion. This would be in keeping with Keynesian theory, which has advocated government intervention in times of need. At the same time, the government should also implement educational and publicity programs to encourage companies to expand and create jobs instead of cutting down jobs and retrenching when implementing automation or cost-reduction. The government should educate everyone concerned, especially the companies and bosses, to take the "macro" view, to realise that retrenchment and unemployment not only affect the employees concerned, but ultimately the whole economy - employers, employees, job-seekers, government, spending/purchasing power, etc., which are all inter-linked; the important point should be made clear to the companies and bosses that rampant retrenchment should be avoided as much as possible, for though it might help the organisation to reduce costs, it is likely to adversely affect staff morale and hence productivity, and, this loss of human productivity would in all likelihood offset the gains of better technology, better equipment (with sabotage of equipment by workers a possible "worst case" situation, which would be reminiscent of the Luddites of the First Industrial Revolution); in other words, besides the hard, technological aspect, an organisation should also pay attention to the soft, human aspect. Only then would new technologies such as automation be looked upon by workers and employees with fond anticipation of job enlargement, promotion, pay increase and higher bonus, rather than fear of being redundant and retrenched, and become really productive.

It should be noted here that new technology comes with the possibility of causing structural unemployment - unemployment resulting from workers being unable to pick up the new skills to take on the newly created jobs in a new industry while loosing their jobs in a declining or "sunset" industry.

However, for society, the economy, as a whole, technology should be their servant; they should not end up being its victim. And, technology should help to boost the economy, e.g., by creating more jobs and increasing the incomes, hence, spending power, of employees, which would be an economic boon, and not take away jobs, retrench, hence reducing purchasing power, which would be a bane for the economy. The obstacle to all this is the unwillingness or inability of workers to undergo skills upgrading and retraining, which is likely to result in some structural unemployment.

In all this, the government has a very important guiding role to play.

10. THE ROLE OF GREED IN THE ECONOMY

Wealth, which is evidently important, is essential for survival and for enjoying the finer things in life. Without money we would not have food, clothing and shelter, let alone the luxuries which only wealth could bring such as entertainment and branded goods. However, too much hankering after wealth and their trappings has apparently insensitised many to the sufferings of others and has created a bunch of self-centred beings, who are competitive, aggressive, arrogant and feel

177

that they have to come up tops in the rat-race. In our advanced, modern society now, many people might have become so materialistic as to be ruthless, and, corrupted even.

Because of materialism, people have rushed into "get-rich-quickly" schemes and scams. Some, because of their greed for wealth, have even been conned into participation in such scams and become swindled of their money. How rich do we want to be? How much money is enough? There seems to be no limit to the yearning for wealth and riches. The more the better, it appears, as far as wealth is concerned.

Of course, the profit motive or the hankering after wealth, i.e., materialism, is the mainstay of a capitalist system such as ours. Economists may argue that this materialism is essential for economic survival and prosperity. Indeed, a person's success or status today tends to be judged by his wealth, whether inherited or acquired. It is little wonder that materialism is continually thriving. People want to earn high salaries for their work and make good profits when they are in business. Thus, job-hopping for greener pastures and profiteering could become the order of the day. Many appear hell-bent on acquiring the five Cs, viz., career, cash, country club membership, car and condominium. Many want to make lots of money and have dared to take the risks of venturing into business. The question is whether without materialism or the profit motive could the economy thrive or even survive? Materialism may be essential to a capitalist system such as ours but could have been played down.

In our pursuit of the material things in life, we may forget that we need calm, peace, security and good companionship with our fellow beings. A highly materialistic society would have many scrambling and competing with each other for wealth and riches, even to the extent of resorting to underhanded tactics such as cheating. It is disturbing to read in the papers that directors and managers of charities siphon off the funds from their charities and rogue lawyers cheat their clients or disappear with their clients' money. This is indeed materialism gone wild or overboard.

Should we then tolerate or condone materialism? Our education system should step in to moderate the thinking of the people, to make the people realise that there are higher, nobler things in life than crass materialism. People should be educated to be moderate, tolerant, cooperative and sympathetic, instead of being crass, ruthless, self-centered and uncooperative. People have not only abandoned their morals, but neglected their health, even their life, in their pursuit of wealth and riches. For example, drug runners still risk their lives in smuggling drugs, a criminal offence which carries the mandatory death sentence in many countries, as they could become rich if successful in their illegal trade.

Is money, wealth or materialism all that one should look forward to in life? The poor who are contented may ultimately be happier (and spiritually richer) than the rich who are never contented. Many of the well-off and rich simply suffer from avarice when they make the worship of money or wealth their creed. Would they really prefer money or wealth over everything else, including their health or even their life? One should really have the correct perspective of things.

In conclusion, we may state that though materialism may be expected of a capitalist system such as ours, we should not allow ourselves to end up as materialism freaks, whereby we become "money-faced" and become obsessed with money and riches to the exclusion of the better, nobler things in life such as harmony, peace and contentment, easier said than done though this may be. The educational system and governmental publicity campaigns could help to inculcate in the people a balanced attitude towards the acquisition of wealth. The "soft" subjects such as philosophy and ethics evidently have an important role in this, and, there should be a new component such as business ethics incorporated into economics, the so-called science of acquiring wealth, and other business subjects. People should be concerned more about moral wealth than material wealth if they really want a happy, harmonious, peaceful society. However, the trend now seems to be gearing towards a society anxious or crazy about getting rich quick through betting, investing in stocks and shares and other "get-rich-quickly" schemes, with white-collar crime, bribery and corruption, adverse financial loss and hardship, and even bankruptcy becoming more common, which is disturbing - wealth being commonly acknowledged the root of all evils. This is evidently the result of society equating wealth with success, with successful business people being given great prominence in the media, making them the objects of envy and emulation. On the other hand, beacons of morality such as Mahatma Gandhi and Mother Theresa should be much the objects of our publicity and emulation. The problem with our capitalistic system is that we need people who are hungry enough for wealth to be willing to undertake the risks of starting businesses which provide employment and products or services for others; i.e., the profit motive plays an important part in the capitalist system, as is stated above. People go after wealth for various reasons, e.g., for survival of course, security, status, power, luxurious living, etc.. It is of course important that there is a proper balance between the acquisition of wealth and moral rectitude. Otherwise, society would in all likelihood end up having more crooks, swindlers, robbers and other social miscreants, an undesirable, fearsome consequence.

The government has an important part to play in bringing about a materially comfortable and morally upright society, in balancing the two well.

11. WHY ECONOMICS DOES NOT SOLVE ECONOMIC PROBLEMS AND WHAT TO DO

Economics can be defined as the science of creating wealth. It is the theoretical underpinning which explains the workings of commerce. The important point to note is that despite the analyses and recommendations of the economic experts who advise, guide and formulate governmental economic policies, the dynamics of the global economy has been as intractable as ever. Governmental policies have always been bandied about to ensure that businesses thrive, people have jobs and the economy is buoyant, but often the reverse results. What can be really seriously affecting the economy? One may wonder.

It should be borne in mind that economics is about the thinking of people involved in commerce - whether they are buying, selling, employing, looking for jobs, trading, negotiating, investing, getting bank loans, lending, etc.. Companies may reduce prices, offer free gifts, increase salaries, provide all kinds of incentives, etc., to attract customers and employees, customers may selectively purchase goods based on brand-name, product image, price, service, or a combination of all these, and workers may choose jobs and employers. To modulate all these commercial activities to ensure that there is prosperity and full employment in the economy, the government has an important, central role. The government, through the central bank, can increase or decrease bank interest rates to encourage or discourage savings and hence reduce or increase the money supply, and, also increase or decrease taxes to reduce or increase the money supply. (The government influences the economy through monetary policies, which pertain to the regulation of money supply, and, fiscal policies, e.g., increasing or lowering taxes and increasing or decreasing spending on public works.)

However, what many seem not to be well aware of is that varying the interest rates and taxation rates by the government quite often do not have the desired effects - increasing or decreasing the money supply, and, increasing or decreasing spending. To expect such governmental economic policies to work all the time is naïve. Such economic policies may work sometimes, but certainly not all the time. To understand why this is so, we need to have a deeper understanding of the human psyche.

Economics is actually ultimately about how people think and behave where money or wealth is concerned. There are many wealthy people who spend relatively little, and even hoard, despite their wealth, while in economic theory we assume that people with more money will spend more. On the other hand, contrary to economic theory, many not so well-off people spend relatively much despite their lack of wealth, and many may even beg, borrow or steal in order to afford a spendthrift, luxurious life-style, e.g., the shopaholics, the night-clubbers, etc.. Though we may expect those with good incomes to save more when bank interest rates are high, this may not happen when the person is spendthrift and generous, e.g., interested in shopping, traveling, dining in fine style, clubbing and giving treats. Some of these people may have other financial commitments, e.g., mortgages to pay, children's education to finance, loans to repay, investments or other business undertakings, etc.; so they may not be able to save despite the high bank interest rates. Of course, those with lower incomes, who are less able to make ends meet, may also not be inclined or able to save even if the bank interest rates were very high.

High import duties and taxes may also not coerce people to spend less. For instance, despite the high import duties, road taxes and ERP charges for cars to discourage car-ownership, making car-ownership in Singapore really expensive, many who can ill afford to own cars possess them, for the love of the automobile, convenience and/or the sake of looking good (status symbol). Despite all the best efforts of the government here to reduce the car population in order to solve the problem of road congestion, car-ownership seems to be getting more robust. And, despite the high import duties and hence high prices of liquor and cigarettes here, those addicted to them evidently continue consuming them as before. We should also not under-estimate the effect of advertising or marketing gimmicks, which can be subtle but can cause impulse buying, especially in the case of consumer products such as food, drinks and clothing - here people who purchase are governed more by emotion or feeling than reason and may do so whimsically.

Also, do not be surprised that often the not so well-off will spend more than the rich. It must be noted that immaterial of whether they are wealthy or poor some people will simply spend, as it is their nature to be spendthrift and generous with money. Some people may just lack financial management skills and discipline where budgeting is concerned while some others are prudent and wise with their money. On the other hand, many wealthy people are miserly or "Jews" as they may be derisively called. That is, the wealthy, who are expected to spend more, or, save more, or, invest, may not do so, while many who are not well-off may spend a great deal, some even borrowing or stealing to do so.

There are also well-to-do people who think far ahead, plan and save for a great future or for the "rainy day" instead of spending freely. There are also people with entrepreneurial ambitions who may save in order to start a business, regardless of the bank interest rates and taxation rates. There are people who live simple lives, who will save a substantial part of their income because they have no interest in shopping, fine-dining, clubbing, traveling and other luxuries.

Doesn't all this explain the frequent failures of governmental monetary and taxation policies where the economy is concerned? Too little money circulating, i.e., too little spending, in the economy leads to depression and unemployment. Too much money circulating, i.e., too much spending, leads to inflation or high prices and financial hardship. However, there is an evident solution to all this. To solve the problem of depression, people can be "forced" to spend in order to increase the money supply and buoy up the economy. Here, two types of currency can be introduced, one type with expiry dates, which may be varied, to ensure that a certain quantity of money circulates during a certain period (these money have to be spent by certain dates and cannot be saved), the other type with no expiry date which can be spent anytime or saved. The expiry dates of the first type of currency can be varied as follows: short, medium or long term in expiry. The expiry dates can be adjusted from time to time according to the economic conditions. For example, if there is inflation, i.e., too much money is in circulation, the currencies with expiry dates may, for instance, specify that the money cannot be spent for the next few months/years (period), after which period they can be spent but will expire on certain dates. By thus playing around with the usage and expiry dates of these currencies, the amount of money, and spending, in the economy can be controlled. On the other hand, to counter the effects of deflation, wherein the quantity of money in circulation and spending are low, the expiry dates of these currencies can be shortened. However, in this instance, to avert the onset of inflation the production of goods and services should keep up with the increased demand caused by the increase in money supply and spending.

All this should be administered by a statutory body or governmental body. Employees and sellers will thus be paid two types of currencies, one with the above-mentioned expiry dates and the other without. What amount or proportion of the two types of currency to be paid out should be determined and administered by this statutory body or governmental body, based on the economic conditions and/or forecasts for the specific period. Neater still if instead of paying by issuing these two types of hard currency a debit card (payment based on the actual amounts of the two types of currency available in the person's debit card account, which will be deducted from the account when the account holder is making payments) is used; this debit card or cashless paying method should make it easier for the governmental institution to administer the whole monetary system. This will apparently be an effective way to overcome our on-going economic malaise over which we seem to have little or no control - depression, unemployment, inflation, deflation. Here we are only talking about monetary transactions within the same country.

At the international level, concerning trading between countries, the same principle should also apply, except that the currencies with expiry dates, the currencies without expiry dates and the debit cards should now be issued and administered by an international authority, e.g., a newly created division of the United Nations. (Please refer to the article, A New Monetary System For Combating Our Economic Ills, in this book.)

Summing up on the point why economics does not solve economic problems, it can be said that economics fail because people's minds, attitudes and behaviours are evidently very difficult, if not impossible, to predict. As is described above, they are complex and come in a great variety of types and characters, often emotional and not very rational, and full of whims and fancies which are quickly changing as well as habits, and therefore cannot be expected to respond appropriately to governmental economic policies which are based on assumptions that may be too simplistic and unrealistic. However, the monetary system described above should perform the trick.

In any case, we should control the economy and not let the economy control us.

SUPPLEMENTARY NOTES ON INFLATION AND UNEMPLOYMENT

The Phillips Curve

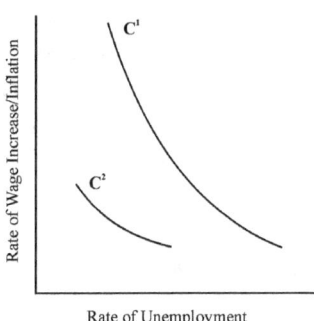

(1) In 1958, A.W. Phillips introduced the Phillips Curve (C^1) which shows that inflation is inversely related to unemployment, i.e., low unemployment leads to high inflation.

(2) In the 70's, 80's and 90's, high inflation and high unemployment (stagflation) persisted.

(3) The Phillips Curve was then modified to C^2.

Okun's Law

(1) The proposition that when the economy picks up after a period of recession the rate of increase in actual output tends to be greater than the rate of decrease in umemployment. (Some of the unemployed or retrenched might not want to rejoin the work-force when the economy picks up.)

(2) Okun puts this ratio at around three for the period 1960 to 1980 in the U.S. economy.

Hyperinflation: Very high inflation, which increases by more than 50% every month.

Stagflation: The situation whereby high inflation and high unemployment persist.

Acceleration Hypothesis (Inflation Expectations): The hypothesis that the expectation that inflation would persist results in wage costs (the result of unions continually pressing for higher and higher wages) and prices (the result of businesses continually increasing prices due to their higher and higher wage bills) spiralling upwards non-stop.

Natural Rate Of Unemployment (NAIRU - Non-accelerating Inflation Rate Of Unemployment):
The underlying rate of unemployment below which it is not possible to reduce unemployment further without increasing the rate of inflation. (Better to have a certain percentage of unemployment in order to prevent inflation.)

Cost-push Inflation:

(i)   Wage-push

(ii) Profit-push

(iii) Tax-push

(iv) Import-price-push

(v)   Exhaustion of natural resources, e.g., short supply of oil results in high price of oil.

Effects Of Inflation (The Details)

(1) Increase or decrease taxes, interest rates and reserve ratios, depending on whether it is demand-pull or cost-push inflation, in order to control money supply.

(2) For demand-pull inflation, government could cause more unemployment (unpopular move by government - political cost).

(3) For cost-push inflation, resort to purchase of cheaper materials or cheaper substitutes.

(4) Workers may press for higher wages through their unions.

(5) Businesses may pass on higher costs to customers in the form of higher prices.

(6) Consumers may purchase less or tighten their belts.

(7) Producers may reduce labour and resort to automation.

(8) Pensioners lose out when their pensions remain fixed though prices have increased.

(9) The lower-income people may moonlight or do side-lines to make ends meet.

(10) The rich may hedge their wealth by investing in properties, commodities and others, e.g., investing in treasury inflation protection securities (TIPS).

(11) May import cheaper goods.

(12) Lenders would lose out, while borrowers gain.

(13) Social problems, e.g., crimes, suicides, divorces, etc..

(14) Exports, due to higher costs, become more expensive and could therefore decline.

(15) Tourist trade is affected badly, due to higher costs and prices, which discourage tourists from visiting the country.

(16) Money could buy less things than before, i.e., real wages are less.

Solution To The Problem Of Stagflation (High Inflation And High Unemployment)

(1) "Supply-side" economics was implemented by the then U.S. president, Ronald Reagan, in 1981 to solve the problem of stagflation.

(2) It advocated low income and capital gains taxes on the wealthy in order to stimulate savings, investment and economic growth.

(3) Such incentive-oriented reductions in taxes expand national output (or supply) more than national demand.

(4) When supply exceeds demand, prices fall and inflation is curbed.

(5) With increasing supply, new jobs would be created, which would reduce unemployment.

(6) The gist of "supply-side" theory is that the government encourages the rich to be productive and innovative through tax handouts and incentives, with the result that inflation and unemployment decrease at the same time.

(7) Also, instead of a deficit in the government budget, the government budget would become balanced, as the incentives generate so much economic growth and income that tax receipts increase greatly in spite of the dwindling taxes.

An Obvious Solution To The Problem Of Persistent Inflation

(1) Common sense says that there should be control or a cap on prices/price increase and wages/wage increase, e.g., by legislation.

(2) Such a policy, or, law, might be difficult to implement and might be unpopular, e.g., the unions might object to and businesses might not welcome the wage curbs and price curbs respectively.

(3) Clearly, the implementation of such a policy, or, legislation, is essential for the prevention of wage-cost spirals and persistent inflation.

(4) In short, the acceleration hypothesis should not have been allowed to become an actuality.

Inflationary Gap:

Excess of total spending (AD) at full employment level of national income, with output remaining the same, while prices increase. (full employment level of national income = potential GNP) To counter the excess in spending, the government could use fiscal and monetary policies.

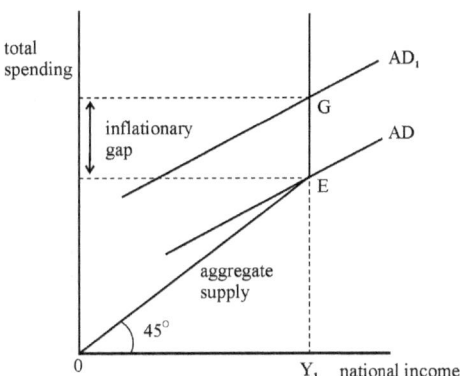

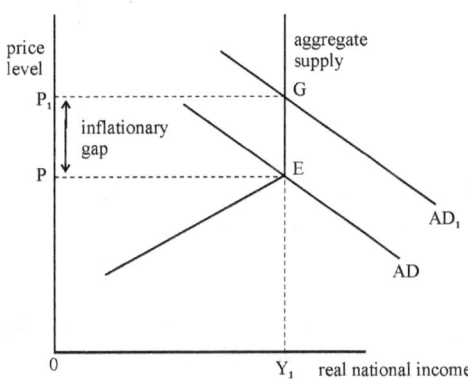

(OY$_1$ = full employment level of national income)

Please Note:

(1) At point E (whence the economy would be operating at full employment), there would not be inflation.

(2) Inflation would occur at point G.

(3) AD$_1$ should be brought down to AD.

(4) Aggregate Supply Schedule is drawn as a 45-degree line because businesses expect AD (aggregate demand) to be just sufficient to sell at that output. At OY$_1$, output cannot increase any more, and Aggregate Supply Schedule becomes vertical.

Deflationary Gap:

Shortfall in total spending (AD) at full employment level of national income (potential GNP), due to a deficiency in spending, with some of the resources in the economy lying idle and actual GNP below that of potential GNP. To counter the deficiency in spending, the government could use fiscal and monetary policies.

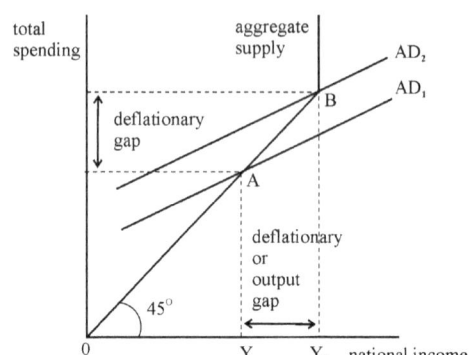

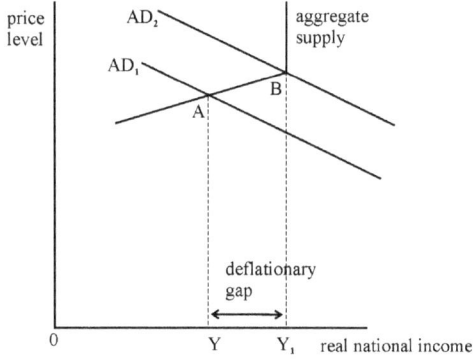

Please Note:

(1) At point B, whence there is full employment of national income (OY_1), actual output cannot expand anymore, and, the Aggregate Supply Schedule becomes vertical.

(2) The actual output would be at A (OY), and is less than potential output at B (OY_1), leaving an output gap.

(3) That is, Actual GNP (OY) is less than Potential GNP (OY_1).

(4) AD_1 should be pushed up to AD_2.

BIBLIOGRAPHY

1) The Wealth Of Nations, *Adam Smith, The Modern Library*

2) The General Theory Of Employment, Interest, And Money, *John Maynard Keynes, Harcourt, Inc.*

3) The Making Of Modern Economics,*Mark Skousen, M. E. Sharpe*

4) Principles Of Economics, *Paul Samuelson, McGraw Hill*

5) Essentials Of Economics, *John Sloman, Prentice Hall*

www.ingramcontent.com/pod-product-compliance
Lightning Source LLC
Chambersburg PA
CBHW072047190526
45165CB00019B/2025